SOCIETY FOR NEW TESTAMENT STUDIES

*MONOGRAPH SERIES*

General Editor: G. N. Stanton

**62**

A BIBLIOGRAPHY OF GREEK
NEW TESTAMENT MANUSCRIPTS

# A Bibliography of Greek New Testament Manuscripts .

**J.K. ELLIOTT**

*Department of Theology, University of Leeds*

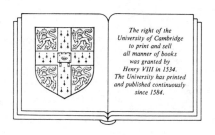

The right of the
University of Cambridge
to print and sell
all manner of books
was granted by
Henry VIII in 1534.
The University has printed
and published continuously
since 1584.

CAMBRIDGE UNIVERSITY PRESS

CAMBRIDGE
NEW YORK   NEW ROCHELLE   MELBOURNE   SYDNEY

Published by the Press Syndicate of the University of Cambridge
The Pitt Building, Trumpington Street, Cambridge CB2 1RP
323 East 57th Street, New York, NY 10022, USA
10 Stamford Road, Oakleigh, Melbourne 3166, Australia

First published 1989

Printed in Great Britain at
the University Press Cambridge


*British Library cataloguing in publication data*

Elliott, J.K. (J. Keith)
A bibliography of Greek New Testament
manuscripts. – (Monograph series/Society for
New Testament studies; 62).
1. Bible. N.T. Greek. Manuscripts.
Bibliographies
I. Title    II. Series
016.2254'8

*Library of Congress cataloguing in publication data*

Elliott, J.K. (James Keith), 1943–
A bibliography of Greek New Testament manuscripts.
(Monographic series / Society for New Testament
Studies; 62)
1. Bible. N.T. – Manuscripts, Greek – Catalogs.
I. Title.    II. Series: Monograph series (Society for
New Testament Studies); 62.
Z7771.M3E43   1988   016.22548   88–9552
[BS1939]

ISBN 0 521 35479 X

To CAROLYN and ROSAMUND

# CONTENTS

# FOREWORD

In the eighteenth century Diderot, the French *Encyclopédiste*, wrote 'Je distingue deux moyens de cultiver les sciences: l'un d'augmenter la masse des connaissances par des découvertes; et c'est ainsi qu'on mérite le nom d'*inventeur*; l'autre de rapprocher les découvertes et de les ordonner entre elles, afin que plus d'hommes soient éclairés, et que chacun participe, selon sa portée, à la lumière de son siècle.' This book, which belongs to Diderot's second category, supplies a much-needed bibliographical tool.

Compiling bibliographies is like fishing with a net. The size of the catch is determined both by the scope of the net and by the tightness of the mesh. Dr Elliott has cast a wide net with narrow mesh, and, consequently, very little that is of importance has escaped his search.

Of the three categories of source materials used in the textual criticism of the New Testament — Greek manuscripts, early versions, patristic quotations — it is, of course, Greek manuscripts that are of primary importance. Now that the sum total of all such witnesses exceeds five thousand, the student (and even the scholar) is often hard put to it to track down information pertaining to a particular manuscript. Although the compiler of this volume disclaims any intent to be exhaustive (an aim that is tantamount to following a will-o'-the wisp), the following pages will prove to be an invaluable aid for many in their scholarly research. Here one finds the titles of books and articles involving editions, facsimiles, and collations, many of which are found in out-of-the-way publications as well as in unpublished theses and dissertations, set forth under the customary categories of papyri, uncials, cursives, and lectionaries. One recalls the truism that a great part of erudition is knowing where to find information: 'Scire ubi aliquid possis invenire magna pars eruditionis est.' Or, according to Alexander Pope's jingling couplet,

> Index-learning turns no student pale,
> Yet holds the Eel of science by the Tail.
> *Dunciad*, I.ii.233 f.

It is said that polite Chinese authors intentionally leave errors in their books in order that the reader, on finding them, may feel superior. Whatever may be thought of such a policy in general, certainly errors in a bibliographical tool, so far from producing feelings of satisfaction, are a source of unmitigated frustration. One expects, however, that in the following pages the compiler, with his customary attention to detail, has managed to keep blind references to a minimum. In any case, however, the reader will be well advised to recollect the Italian proverb, 'Chi non falla non fa.'

Princeton, New Jersey                           BRUCE M. METZGER

# ABBREVIATIONS

## Journals and series

| | |
|---|---|
| *AJP* | *American Journal of Philology* (Baltimore, 1880– ) |
| *AJT* | *American Journal of Theology* (Chicago, 1897–1920) |
| *Amer J Arch* | *American Journal of Archaeology* (Princeton, 1885–96; Second Series, Norwood, Mass., 1897– ) |
| *Anal Boll* | *Analecta Bollandiana* (Brussels, 1882– ) |
| *APF* | *Archiv für Papyrusforschung* (Berlin, 1901– 41, 1953– ) |
| *ATR* | *Anglican Theological Review* (New York, 1918– ) |
| AUSS | Andrews University Seminary Series (Berrien Springs, Mich., 1963– ) |
| *BBC* | *Bulletin of the Bezan Club* (Leiden, 1925–37) |
| *Bib Arch* | *Biblical Archaeologist* (New Haven, 1938– ) |
| *BJRL* | *Bulletin of the John Rylands Library* (Manchester, 1903– ) |
| *BMQ* | *British Museum Quarterly* (London, 1926– ) |
| *Bull Soc Arch Copte* | *Bulletin de la Société d'Archéologie copte* (Cairo, 1938– ) |
| *Byz Z* | *Byzantinische Zeitschrift* (Leipzig, 1892– ) |
| *BZ* | *Biblische Zeitschrift* (Paderborn, 1903–39; N.S., 1957– ) |
| *BZNW* | *Beihefte zur Zeitschrift für die neutestamentliche Wissenschaft* (Berlin, 1923– ) |
| *EE* | *Estudios ecclesiasticos* (Madrid, 1922–36, 1942– ) |
| *Emérita* | *Emérita: Rivista de linguística y filología clásica* (Madrid, 1933– ) |

| | |
|---|---|
| *ET* | *Expository Times* (Edinburgh, 1889– ) |
| *Ex* | *Expositor* (London) |
| | First Series 1875–80 |
| | Second Series 1881–4 |
| | Third Series 1885–9 |
| | Fourth Series 1890–4 |
| | Fifth Series 1895–9 |
| | Sixth Series 1900–5 |
| | Seventh Series 1906–10 |
| | Eighth Series 1911–23 |
| | Ninth Series 1924–5 |
| *Fo und Fo* | *Forschungen und Fortschritte* (Berlin, 1925–67) |
| *Helmantica* | *Helmantica: Rivista de humanidades clásicas* (Salamanca, 1950– ) |
| *HLS* | *Historical and Linguistic Studies in Literature related to the New Testament* (Chicago) |
| *HTR* | *Harvard Theological Review* (Cambridge, Mass., 1908– ) |
| *HTS* | *Harvard Theological Studies* (Cambridge, Mass., 1916– ) |
| *ICC* | *International Critical Commentary* (Edinburgh, 1895– ) |
| *Jahr öster byz Gesell* | *Jahrbuch der österreichischen byzantinischen Gesellschaft* (Vienna, 1951– ) |
| *JBL* | *Journal of Biblical Literature* (Philadelphia, 1881– ) |
| *JHS* | *Journal of Hellenic Studies* (London, 1880– ) |
| *J of Phil* | *Journal of Philology* (London, 1868–1920) |
| *JR* | *Journal of Religion* (Chicago, 1921– ) |
| *JSNT* | *Journal for the Study of the New Testament* (Sheffield, 1978– ) |
| *JTS* | *Journal of Theological Studies* (Oxford, 1899– ) |
| *Mo* | *Monist* (Chicago, 1890– ) |
| *Muséon* | *Le Muséon* (Louvain, 1882–1915, 1921– ) |
| *Nov T* | *Novum Testamentum* (Leiden, 1956– ) |
| *NTS* | *New Testament Studies* (Cambridge, 1954– ) |
| *NTTS* | *New Testament Tools and Studies* (Leiden, 1950– ) |

| | |
|---|---|
| *Oriens Christ* | *Oriens Christianus* (Rome, 1901–11<br>New Series 1911–24<br>Third Series 1921–39<br>Fourth Series 1953– ) |
| *PSI* | *Pubblicazioni della Società Italiana* (Papiri<br>Greci e Latini)<br>(Florence, 1912– )<br>vols. 1–11, ed. G. Vitelli<br>vol. 12, ed. M. Norsa and V. Bartoletti<br>vol. 13, ed. M. Norsa<br>vol. 14, ed. V. Bartoletti |
| *R Bén* | *Revue Bénédictine* (Maredsous, 1890– ) |
| *RE* | *Review and Expositor* (Louisville, 1904– ) |
| *Rev bib* | *Revue biblique* (Paris, 1892– ) |
| *RR* | *Ricerche religiose* (Rome, 1925–33, 1947–9) |
| *RSR* | *Recherches de science religieuse* (Paris, 1910– ) |
| *S & D* | *Studies and Documents* |
| *Sitzb Berl Akad* | *Sitzungsberichte der preussischen Akademie<br>der Wissenschaften* (Berlin, 1882– ) |
| *SNTS* | *Studiorum Novi Testamenti Societas* mono-<br>graph series (Cambridge) |
| *Sp* | *Speculum: A Journal of Medieval Studies*<br>(Cambridge, Mass., 1926– ) |
| *Stud zur Pal und<br>    Pap* | *Studien zur Paläographie und Papyruskunde*,<br>ed. C. Wessely (Leipzig)<br>Reference is to vol. 9 (1909); vol. 11 (1911);<br>vol. 12 (1912); vol. 15 (1914); vol. 18 (1917) |
| *Stud pap* | *Studia papyrologica* (Barcelona, 1962– ) |
| *T & U* | *Texte und Untersuchungen zur Geschichte der<br>altchristlichen Literatur* (Berlin, 1882– ) |
| *Th Lit* | *Theologische Literaturblatt* (Leipzig, 1880–<br>1943) |
| *Th Q* | *Theologische Quartalschrift* (Tübingen,<br>1818– ) |
| *TLZ* | *Theologische Literaturzeitung* (Leipzig,<br>1876–1944, 1947– ) |
| *TM* | *Theological Monthly* (Lutheran Synod)<br>(St Louis, Mo., 1921– ) |
| *TZ* | *Theologische Zeitschrift* (Basle, 1945– ) |
| *Vet Chr* | *Vetera Christianorum* (Bari, 1964– ) |

| | |
|---|---|
| *Wien Stud* | *Wiener Studien, Zeitschrift für klassische Philologie* (Vienna, 1897– ) |
| *ZBW* | *Zentralblatt* [originally *Centralblatt*] *für Bibliothekswesen* (Leipzig, 1884– ) |
| *ZNW* | *Zeitschrift für die neutestamentliche Wissenschaft* (Berlin, 1900– ) |
| *ZPE* | *Zeitschrift für Papyrologie und Epigraphik* (Bonn, 1967– ) |

All other journals and series are set out in full in the bibliography.


## Books

The following are referred to in the bibliography in an abbreviated form, as indicated in the left-hand column below:

| | |
|---|---|
| A & A | K. Aland and B. Aland, *Der Text des Neuen Testaments* (Stuttgart, 1982; ET Grand Rapids, 1986) |
| Aland, *Repertorium* | K. Aland (ed.), *Repertorium der Griechischen Christlichen Papyri* I, *Biblische Papyri, Patristische Texte und Studien* 18 (Berlin/New York, 1976) |
| Amélineau, *Notice* | E. Amélineau, *Notice des manuscrits coptes de la Bibliothèque Nationale* (*Notices et extraits* 34, 2) (Paris, 1895), pp. 363–427 |
| *ANTF* 3 | K. Aland (ed.), *Materialien zur neutestamentlichen Handschriftenkunde, Arbeiten zur neutestamentliche Textforschung* III (Berlin/New York, 1969) |
| *ANTF* 6 | K. Junack and W. Grunewald (eds.), *Das Neue Testament auf Papyrus: I Die Katholischen Briefe, Arbeiten zur neutestamentlichen Textforschung* VI (Berlin/New York, 1986) (A collation of the following papyri: P 9, 20, 23, 54, 72, 74, 78, 81) |
| *ANTF* 7 | B. Aland (ed.), *Das Neue Testament in syrischer Überlieferung: I Die Grossen Katholischen Briefe, Arbeiten zur neutestamentlichen Textforschung* VII (Berlin/New York, 1986) |

(Includes detailed discussion and collation of four minuscules allegedly behind the Harclean Syriac version, viz. cursives 1505, 1611, 2138, 2495)

Barbour  R. Barbour, *Greek Literary Hands A.D. 400–600, Oxford Palaeographical Handbook* (Oxford, 1981)

Beginnings of  F.J. Foakes Jackson and K. Lake (eds.),
Christianity  *The Beginnings of Christianity*, pt I, *The Acts of the Apostles* (5 vols., London, 1920–33)

Beneševič II  V. Beneševič, *Monumenta Sinaitica*, II (St Petersburg, 1912)

Bianchini, *Evang*  G. Bianchini, *Evangeliarium quadruplex*
*quadr*  (Rome, 1749)

Bick  J. Bick, *Die Schreiber der Wiener Griechischen Handschriften, Museion Abhandlungen* I (Vienna, 1920)

Cavalieri and  P. Franchi de' Cavalieri and J. Lietzmann,
Lietzmann  *Specimina codicum Graecorum Vaticanorum* (Bonn, 1910)

Cavallo  G. Cavallo, *Richerche sulla maiuscola biblica* (Florence, 1967)

Cereteli and  S. Cereteli and S. Sobolewski, *Exempla*
Sobolewski  *codicum Graecorum litteris minusculis scriptorum* (2 vols., Moscow, 1911–13)

Clark F/S  B.L. Daniels and M.J. Suggs (eds.), *Studies in the History and Text of the New Testament in honor of K.W. Clark*, S & D 29 (Salt Lake City, 1967)

Clark, *USA*  K.W. Clark, *A Descriptive Catalogue of Greek New Testament Manuscripts in America* (Chicago, 1937)
(Plates shown as Clark and page number)

Colwell, *Four*  E. Colwell, *The Four Gospels of Karahissar*,
Gospels  2 vols. I, *History and Text* (Chicago, 1936); (vol. II by H. Willoughby is on art and ornamentation)

von Dobschütz  E. Nestle, *Einführung in das griechische Neue Testament*, 4th edn, revised by E. von Dobschütz (Göttingen, 1923)

Finegan  J. Finegan, *Encountering New Testament Manuscripts* (London, 1975)

| | |
|---|---|
| Follieri | H. Follieri, *Codices Graeci Bibliothecae Vaticanae selecti ..., Exempla Scripturarum* IV (Vatican, 1969) |
| Furlan | I. Furlan, *Codici Greci illustrati della Biblioteca Marciana* (Milan, I, 1978, II, 1979, III, 1980) |
| Graux and Martin | C. Graux and A. Martin, *Fac-Similés de manuscrits grecs d'Espagne* (Paris, 1891) |
| Gregory, *Textkritik* | C.R. Gregory, *Textkritik des Neuen Testamentes* (3 vols., Leipzig, 1900–9) |
| Hansell | E.H. Hansell, *Novum Testamentum Graece*, 3 vols. (Oxford, 1864) |
| Harlfinger *et al.* | D. Harlfinger, D.R. Reinsch and J.A.M. Sonderkamp, *Specimina Sinaitica* (Berlin, 1983) |
| Hatch, *Jer* | W.H.P. Hatch, *The Greek Manuscripts of the New Testament in Jerusalem: Facsimiles and Descriptions* (Paris, 1934) |
| Hatch (in list of cursives) | W.H.P. Hatch, *Facsimiles and descriptions of minuscule manuscripts of the New Testament* (Cambridge, Mass., 1951) For lectionaries the volume is identified as *Mins* |
| Hatch (in lists of papyri and uncials) | W.H.P. Hatch, *The Principal Uncial Manuscripts of the New Testament* (Chicago, 1939) For lectionaries the volume is identified as *Uncials* |
| Hatch, *Sinai* | W.H.P. Hatch, *The Greek Manuscripts of the New Testament at Mount Sinai: Facsimiles and Descriptions* (Paris, 1932) |
| Horner, *Sahidic* | G. Horner, *The Coptic Version of the New Testament in the Southern Dialect* (7 vols., Oxford, 1911–24) |
| Horsley, pp. 125–40 | G.H.R. Horsley, *New Documents Illustrating Early Christianity* 2 (Macquarie University, 1982), pp. 125–40 (reprinting the text of one papyrus and twelve uncials) |
| Hoskier, *Text* | H.C. Hoskier, *Concerning the Text of the Apocalypse* (2 vols., London, 1929) References are to vol. I and page number; but all collations are given in vol. II |

| | |
|---|---|
| Hutter | I. Hutter, *Corpus der byzantinischen Miniaturhandschriften*, I, *Oxford, Bodleian Library*, I (Stuttgart, 1977) |
| Kenyon, *Facsimiles* | F.G. Kenyon, *Facsimiles of Biblical Manuscripts in the British Museum* (London, 1900) |
| Kenyon (1912) | F.G. Kenyon, *Handbook to the Textual Criticism of the New Testament*, 2nd edn, (London, 1912) |
| Kenyon/Adams | F.G. Kenyon, *The Text of the Greek Bible*, 3rd edn revised by A.W. Adams (London, 1975) |
| Kenyon–Adams, *Our Bible* | F.G. Kenyon, *Our Bible and the Ancient Manuscripts*, 5th edn revised by A.W. Adams (London, 1958) |
| Lake and Lake | *Dated Greek Minuscule Manuscripts to the Year 1200*, ed. Kirsopp Lake and Silva Lake (10 vols., Boston, Mass., 1934–9), *Monumenta and Palaeographica vetera* First Series, and *Indexes, vols. I to X* (Boston, Mass., 1945) (Reference is to the number allocated to the MS by the editors and not to the number of the plate(s). For some MSS more than one plate is to be found) |
| Lake F/S | *Quantulacumque: Studies Presented to Kirsopp Lake by Pupils, Colleagues and Friends*, ed. Robert P. Casey, Silva Lake and Agnes K. Lake (London, 1937) |
| Lefort and Cochez | L.T. Lefort and J. Cochez, *Philologische Studien: Palaeographisch Album, Tijdschrift voor classieke Philologie-Albumreeks*, I (Louvain, 1932–4) |
| Matthaei | C.F. Matthaei, *Novum Testamentum Graece et Latine* (Riga, 1782–8) (The sigla used by Matthaei are given) |
| Metzger, *Manuscripts* | B.M. Metzger, *Manuscripts of the Greek Bible* (Oxford and New York, 1981) |
| Metzger, *Text* | B.M. Metzger, *The Text of the New Testament*, 2nd edn (Oxford, 1968) |
| Milligan | G. Milligan, *The New Testament Documents: their Origin and Early History* (London, 1913) |
| Montfaucon | B. Montfaucon, *Biblioteca Coisliniana* (Paris, 1715) |

| | |
|---|---|
| Muralt, *NT Gr* | E. Muralt, *Novum Testamentum Graece* (Hamburg, 1848) |
| Naldini, *Documenti* | M. Naldini, *Documenti dell'Antichità Cristiana*, 2nd edn (Florence, 1965) |
| New Pal Soc | *Facsimiles of Ancient Manuscripts*, ed. E. M. Thompson and others, I (London, 1903–12); II (London, 1913–34) |
| Omont (1896) | H. Omont, *Très anciens manuscrits grecs bibliques et classiques de la Bibliothèque Nationale* (Paris, 1896) |
| Omont, *Facs* (1891) | H. Omont, *Fac-similés des manuscrits grecs datés de la Bibliothèque Nationale du IXe and XIVe siècle* (Paris, 1891) |
| Omont, *Facs* (1892) | H. Omont, *Fac-similés des plus anciens mss. grecs de la Bibliothèque Nationale du IVe and XIIIe siècle* (Paris, 1892) |
| *OP* | *Oxyrhynchus Papyri* (London, 1892–  ). The editors' names and the volume numbers are given. The dates of volumes containing NT material are: |

| | | | |
|---|---|---|---|
| I | (1892) | II | (1899) |
| III | (1903) | IV | (1908) |
| V | (1908) | VII | (1910) |
| VIII | (1911) | IX | (1912) |
| X | (1914) | XI | (1915) |
| XIII | (1919) | XV | (1922) |
| XVI | (1924) | XVIII | (1941) |
| XXIV | (1957) | XXXIV | (1968) |
| L | (1983) | | |

| | |
|---|---|
| Pal Soc | *Facsimiles of Manuscripts and Inscriptions*, ed. E. A. Bond, E. M. Thompson and others, I (London, 1873–83); II (London, 1884–94) |
| Pap di Firenze | I. Crisci, 'La Collezione dei papiri di Firenze', in *Proceedings of the Twelfth International Congress of Papyrologists* (Toronto, 1970), pp. 89–95 |
| Pattie | T. S. Pattie, *Manuscripts of the Bible* (London, 1979) |
| *RGG* | *Die Religion in Geschichte und Gegenwart*, 1st edn (Tübingen, 1909–13) |
| Sabas | K. Sabas (Savva), *Specimina palaeographia* |

|  | cod. Graecorum et Slavonicorum (Moscow, 1863) |
|---|---|
| Schmid | J. Schmid, *Studien zur Geschichte des Griechischen Apokalypse-Textes*, 3 vols., *Münchener Theologische Studien* (Munich, 1955–6) |
| Schofield | E. M. Schofield, 'The Papyrus Fragments of the Greek New Testament', Unpublished Ph.D. thesis, Southern Baptist Theological Seminary, Louisville, Ky, 1936 |
| Scrivener (1859) | F. H. A. Scrivener, *Contributions to the Criticism of the Greek New Testament* (Cambridge and London, 1859) |
| Scrivener, *Adversaria* | F. H. A. Scrivener, *Adversaria critica sacra* (Cambridge, 1893) |
| Scrivener, *Exact Transcript* | F. H. A. Scrivener, *An Exact Transcript of the Codex Augiensis* (Cambridge and London, 1859) |
| Scrivener, *Full and Exact Collation* | F. H. A. Scrivener, *A Full and Exact Collation of About 20 Greek Manuscripts of the Holy Gospels* (Cambridge and London, 1852) |
| Scrivener, *Intr* | F. H. A. Scrivener, *A Plain Introduction to the Textual Criticism of the New Testament* (3rd edn, London, 1883); (4th edn, London, 1894) |
| Seider | R. Seider, *Paläographie der griechischen Papyri* (Stuttgart, vol. I, 1967; II, 1970) |
| Silvestre | J. B. Silvestre, *Paléographie universelle* (Paris, 1839–41) |
| Sitterly (1898) | C. F. Sitterly, *Praxis in Manuscripts of the Greek Testament*, 2nd edn (New York and Cincinnati, 1898) |
| Sitterly (1914) | C. F. Sitterly, *The Canon, Text and Manuscripts of the New Testament, illustrated with Tables, Facsimile Plates and Survey of the Earliest Mss.* (New York, 1914) |
| *Six Collations* | *Six Collations of New Testament Manuscripts*, ed. K. Lake and S. New, *HTS* 17 (Cambridge, Mass., and London, 1932) |
| Tischendorf, *Anecdota* | C. Tischendorf, *Anecdota sacra et profana*, 2nd edn (Leipzig, 1861) |
| Tischendorf, *Mon sac* (with date) | C. Tischendorf, *Monumenta sacra inedita* (Leipzig, 1846) |

| | |
|---|---|
| Tischendorf, *Mon sac* (with date or volume number) | C. Tischendorf, *Monumenta sacra inedita (Nova collectio)* (Leipzig) Vol. I (1855) II (1857) III (1860) V (1865) VI (1869) IX (1870) |
| Tischendorf, *Notitia* | C. Tischendorf, *Notitia editionis codicis Bibliorum Sinaitici* (Leipzig, 1860) |
| Treu | Kurt Treu, *Die Griechischen Handschriften des Neuen Testaments in der UdSSR; eine systematische Auswertung des Texthandschriften in Leningrad, Moskau, Kiev, Odessa, Tbilisi und Erevan, T & U* 91 (Berlin, 1966) |
| Treu, *Bilinguen* | 'Griechisch-koptische Bilinguen des Neuen Testaments', in *Koptische Studien in der DDR*, edited by the Institut für Byzantinistik (Halle, 1965), pp. 95–123 |
| Turyn (1964) | A. Turyn, *Codices Graeci Vaticani saeculis XIII et XIV scripti, Codices e Vaticanis selecti* 28 (Vatican, 1964) |
| Turyn (1972) | A. Turyn, *Dated Greek Manuscripts of the Thirteenth and Fourteenth Centuries in the Libraries of Italy* 2 vols. (Urbana, 1972) |
| Turyn, *GB* | A. Turyn, *Dated Greek Manuscripts of the Thirteenth and Fourteenth Centuries in the Libraries of Great Britain*, Dumbarton Oaks Series XVII (Washington, D.C., 1980) |
| Vikan | G. Vikan (ed.), *Illuminated Greek Mss. from American Collections* (Princeton University, 1973) |
| Vogels | H. J. Vogels, *Codicum Novi Testamenti specimina* (Bonn, 1929) |
| Wessely, *Patr or* | C. Wessely (ed.), 'Les Plus Anciens Monuments du Christianisme écrits sur papyrus', in *Patrologia orientalis* vol. IV, 2 (Paris, 1907); vol. XVIII, 3 (Paris, 1924) (For papyri 1, 3, 5, 10, 15, 16, 17, 18, 20, 22, 23, 24, 27) |
| Wilson | N. G. Wilson, *Medieval Greek Bookhands* 2 vols. (Cambridge, Mass., 1972 and 1973) |

| Wilson and Stefanović | N.G. Wilson and D.I. Stefanović, *Manuscripts of Byzantine Chant in Oxford* (Oxford, 1963) |
| Wittek | M. Wittek, *Album de paléographie grecque* (Ghent, 1967) |

# INTRODUCTION

To compile an exhaustive bibliography on New Testament Greek manuscripts, in which all articles, books and plates on every aspect of each manuscript would find a place, seems to me to be not only impossible but also unnecessary. I have therefore limited the scope of this bibliography by having in mind a particular type of reader, namely a student of the Greek New Testament rather than a librarian. What I hope I have provided is a useful and reliable tool for the reader who is interested in a particular manuscript of the New Testament and wishes to see if it is published as a facsimile, or if a photographic reproduction or collation is available, or if a major study of its textual character has been undertaken.

I have therefore not been concerned to satisfy those whose interest in manuscripts is in their art-work, miniatures, illuminations, etc., nor have I been concerned to include all references to the history of a given manuscript. I have likewise tended to exclude references to short notes in learned journals that treat of an isolated reading in a single manuscript or group of manuscripts, although it may well be that the student who turns to this bibliography to search for further studies on a manuscript has had his attention drawn to that manuscript by such a short note, or by a striking variant in a critical apparatus.

Library catalogue descriptions have, for the most part, been excluded, although I have made exceptions in the case of descriptive catalogues published by those whose interest is in textual criticism in general and New Testament textual criticism in particular, such as K. W. Clark on New Testament manuscripts in the U.S.A., or K. Treu on New Testament manuscripts in the U.S.S.R. I have also included references to M.-J. Lagrange's brief but often helpful descriptions. Reference to earlier catalogues by, say, Coxe[1] of the Bodleian

---

[1] H. O. Coxe, *Catalogi codicum mss. Bibliothecae Bodleianae* (Oxford, 1853).

manuscripts, or Omont[2] of the Paris collections made by C.R. Gregory in his *Prolegomena* to the 8th edition of Tischendorf's *Novum Testamentum Graece* (Leipzig, 1894) did not seem to be worth reproducing here. Those whose interests lie in these directions will turn to M. Richard, *Répertoire des bibliothèques et des catalogues de manuscrits grecs*, 2nd edn (CNRS, Paris, 1958), and id., *Supplément I 1958–63* (CNRS, Paris, 1964).[3]

References to manuscripts in sale-room or exhibition catalogues have in general been ignored, partly for the same reason that library catalogue entries have been omitted, but also partly because of the general inaccessibility of such sources.

It is assumed that in addition to the present bibliography, information on a particular manuscript will be sought in the current registers of New Testament manuscripts published by the internationally recognised registrar, K. Aland. His lists give basic details about the age, contents, dimensions, writing material, number of lines per page, number of columns per page and the library catalogue number for each manuscript that has been allocated a Gregory-Aland number. The lists may be found in:

> K. Aland, *Kurzgefasste Liste der griechischen Handschriften des Neuen Testaments* I, *Gesamtübersicht*, *Arbeiten zur Neutestamentlichen Textforschung* I (Berlin/New York, 1963).[4]

A revision of this work is being undertaken. In the meantime, *addenda* and *corrigenda* to this volume may be found in

---

[2] H. Omont, *Inventaire sommaire des manuscrits grecs de la Bibliothèque Nationale* (Paris, 1886–8); id., *Inventaire sommaire des manuscrits grecs conservés dans les bibliothèques publiques de Paris autres que la Bibliothèque Nationale* (Paris, 1883); cf. J.P.P. Martin, *Description technique des manuscrits grecs relatifs au Nouveau Testament conservés dans les bibliothèques de Paris* (Paris, 1884).

[3] Additional material, particularly on special collections, may be seen in the British Museum *Catalogue of Additions 1756–1782* (London, 1977); S. and S. Eustratiades, *Catalogue of the Greek Manuscripts in the Library of the Laura on Mount Athos with Notices from other Libraries*, *HTS* 12 (Cambridge, Mass., 1925; reprinted 1969 by Kraus Reprint); K.W. Clark, *Checklist of Manuscripts in St. Catherine's Monastery, Mount Sinai: microfilmed for the Library of Congress, 1950* (Washington, Library of Congress Photoduplication Services, 1952).

[4] Papyri: 1–76  Uncials: 01–0250  Cursives: 1–2646  Lectionaries: *l*1–*l*1997.

K. Aland, 'Die griechischen Handschriften des Neuen Testaments. Ergänzungen zur "Kurzgefasste Liste" (Fortsetzungsliste VII)', in K. Aland (ed.), *Materialien zur Neutestamentlichen Handschriften* I, *Arbeiten zur Neutestamentlichen Textforschung* III) (Berlin/New York, 1969), pp. 22–37;[5]

*Bericht der Stiftung zur Förderung der Neutestamentlichen Textforschung für die Jahre 1970 und 1971* (Münster, 1972), pp. 13–21;[6]

*Bericht der Stiftung zur Förderung der Neutestamentlichen Textforschung für die Jahre 1972 bis 1974* (Münster, 1974), pp. 9–13;[7] and

*Bericht der Stiftung zur Förderung der Neutestamentlichen Textforschung für die Jahre 1975 und 1976* (Münster, 1977), pp. 11–16.[8]

The details provided in Aland's lists are not as full as those found in some earlier descriptions (*Kurzgefasste Liste* II, *Einzelübersichten*, originally proposed by K. Aland, is not now to appear). This means that, for some manuscripts, additional information, and sometimes bibliographical details, may be found in older publications. A useful starting-point is Gregory's *Prolegomena*, which gives references to existing library catalogues and also to early collations or classifications by Wettstein, Griesbach, and Scholz, and to early descriptions by, for example, Montfaucon. I have not generally reproduced such information as it is easily accessible in Gregory and much of it is of only antiquarian interest. I have made an exception in the case of both Scrivener and Matthaei: manuscripts known to and used by them in their Greek New Testaments are identified in the bibliography because fairly reliable early collations (in some cases the *only* published collations) may be gleaned from their apparatus.[9]

---

[5] Papyri: 77–81
Uncials: 0251–0267
Cursives: 2647–2768
Lectionaries: *l*1998–*l*2146.

[6] Cursives: 2769–2792
Lectionaries: *l*2147–*l*2193.

[7] Papyri: 82, 86
Uncials: 0268–0269
Cursives: 2793–2795
Lectionaries: *l*2194–*l*2207.

[8] Papyri: 85, 87, 88
Uncials: 0270–0274
Lectionaries: *l*2208–*l*2209.

[9] Help in identifying some of Scrivener's MSS may be had in S. Kubo, 'Identification of Scrivener's Collated Manuscripts', AUSS 16 (1978), 297–400.

H. von Soden, *Die Schriften des Neuen Testaments* (Berlin/ Göttingen, 1902–13) also includes descriptive lists of the manuscripts he uses (especially in I 1), together with descriptions of their textual worth according to his textual theories (especially in I 2 and 3). Similarly, short descriptions of manuscripts may be seen in vol. I of F. H. A. Scrivener, *A Plain Introduction to the Criticism of the New Testament*, 4th edn revised by E. Miller (London/New York/ Cambridge, 1894).

Excluding von Soden (whose classification of manuscripts differs from that now universally accepted) the increasing length of the list of officially recognised New Testament manuscripts may be seen by tracing the growth from the time of Gregory's *Prolegomena* through the latest additions to Aland's *Liste* in the Münster *Bericht* of 1977. (Since then, of course, the list has grown even longer, and references to manuscripts with a higher number than those recorded at that time may be found in this bibliography.) This information is now provided not only for historic interest, but because greater detail is sometimes to be found in the first publication or notification of a manuscript's existence than in later publications.

The inauguration of the current (Gregory) numeration may be found in C. R. Gregory, *Die Griechischen Handschriften des Neuen Testaments, Versuche und Entwürfe* 2 (Leipzig, 1908) with descriptions of the following manuscripts:

> Papyri: 1–14
> Uncials: 01–0161
> Cursives: 1–2293 (and 2293–2034 in the *Nachtrag*)
> Lectionaries: *l*1–*l*1540 (and *l*1541–*l*1547 and a few others in the *Nachtrag*).

The third volume of C. R. Gregory, *Textkritik des Neuen Testamentes* (Leipzig, 1900–9), published in 1909, increased these numbers:

> (Papyri: 1–14)
> Uncials: 01–0166
> Cursives: 1–2318
> Lectionaries: *l*1–*l*1561 (and a few others).

The listing continued in the following publications:

> C. R. Gregory, 'Vorschläge für eine kritische Ausgabe des Griechischen Neuen Testaments', in *Versuche und Entwürfe* 5 (Leipzig, 1911), pp. 34–6:

Uncials: 0162–0168
Cursives: 2305–2320
Lectionaries: *l*1548–*l*1561;

C. R. Gregory, 'Griechische Handschriften des Neuen
Testaments bis zum 1 Juli 1912', *TLZ* 37 (1912),
col. 477:
Papyri: 15–19
Uncials: 0167–0169
Cursives: 2308–2326
Lectionaries: *l*1562–*l*1565.

After Gregory's death the listing was continued by E. von Dobschütz,
whose contributions included *addenda* and *corrigenda* to previously
published lists, as well as introducing the following new manuscripts
in his revision of Nestle's Introduction:

E. Nestle, *Einführung in das griechische Neue
Testament*, 4th edn revised by E. von Dobschütz
(Göttingen, 1923), pp. 86 and 97:
Papyri: 20–32
Talismans: 1–2
Uncial: 0170.

Thereafter, von Dobschütz's contributions appeared in *ZNW* under
the series title 'Zur Liste der Neutestamentlichen Handschriften':

I *ZNW* 23 (1924), 248–64
Papyri: 33–36
Uncials: 0171–0188
Cursives: 2327–2354
Lectionaries: *l*1566–*l*1580
II *ZNW* 25 (1926), 299–306
Papyri: 37–39
Talismans: 3–4
Cursives: 2355–2357
Lectionaries: *l*1590–*l*1595
III *ZNW* 27 (1928), 216–22
Papyri: 40–41
Talismans: 5–6
Uncial: 0189
Cursives: 2358–2359

IV *ZNW* 32 (1933), 185–206
  Papyri: 42–48
  Ostraca[10]: 1–25
  Talismans[10]: 7–9
  Uncials: 0190–0208
  Cursives: 2360–2362, 2394–2401
  Lectionaries: *l*1597–*l*1609.

This series lapsed until it was revived by K. Aland in 1954 (see below). In the meantime the following were published:

> G. Maldfeld, 'Die Griechischen Handschriftenbruch-stücke des Neuen Testamentes auf Papyrus', *ZNW* 42 (1949), 228–53, with *addenda* and *corrigenda* in *ZNW* 43 (1950–1), 260–1:
> Papyri: 42–62;

> K. Aland, 'Zur Liste der Griechischen Neutestament-lichen Handschriften', *TLZ* 75 (1950), cols. 58–60:
> Papyri: 25, 42, 51, 55–62;

> K. Aland, 'Zur Liste der Griechischen Neutestament-lichen Handschriften', *TLZ* 78 (1953), cols. 465–96:
> Papyrus: 63
> Uncials: 0209–0232
> Cursives: 2363–2393, 2395, 2402–2440[11]
> Lectionaries: *l*1610–*l*1678.

In 1954 Aland continued the series 'Zur Liste der Neutestamentlichen Handschriften':

> V *ZNW* 45 (1954), 179–217
>   Papyrus: 64
>   Uncials: 0209–0239
>   Cursives: 2441–2491
>   Lectionaries: *l*1679–*l*1748
> VI *ZNW* 48 (1957), 141–91
>   Papyri: 65–68

---

[10] These categories are now no longer continued.
[11] Misprinted as 2340 (col. 484).

Uncials: 0240–0241
Cursives: 2492–2533
Lectionaries: *l*1749–*l*1838.
VII occurs in *ANTF* III (see above).

For an analysis and survey of each manuscript that is to be found in the critical apparatus of recent major editions of the Greek New Testament and the Synoptic Gospels my *A Survey of Manuscripts used in Editions of the Greek New Testament, Novum Testamentum Supplements* 57 (Leiden, 1987), may be of help.

As far as references to plates are concerned,[12] I have tried to limit these to collections of plates of text in works by textual critics such as the Lakes, Hatch, and Metzger, whose works usually include helpful explanatory notes on each reproduction they print, but I have also included material in such major series as the Palaeographical Society's fascicles. Generally, references to plates included in works earlier than 1900 have not been given because the reproductions are not usually of high definition, nor are the publications themselves easily accessible. I have ignored plates that show only a superscription or an artist's illustration. For these I have provided a cross-reference (Plates*): this means that bibliographical material is to be found in S. J. Voicu and S. d'Alisera, *Index in manuscriptorum Graecorum edita specimina* (Rome, 1981) (often known as *IMAGES*).[13]

For most of the manuscripts that contain the Book of Revelation H. C. Hoskier's monumental two-volume work *Concerning the Text of the Apocalypse* (London, 1929) provides a collation and description. References throughout the bibliography are to the descriptions of manuscripts in his first volume: the collations occur in volume 2. For manuscripts of the Book of Revelation, reference ought also be made to J. Schmid, *Studien zur Geschichte des griechischen Apokalypse-Textes* (2 vols., Munich, 1955–6), where manuscripts are grouped in accordance with Schmid's textual analyses. (See also his 'Untersuchungen zur Geschichte des griechischen Apokalypsetextes', *Biblica* XVII (1936), 11–44, 167–201, 273–93, 429–60.)

Reviews of important books on individual manuscripts have been given occasionally when they seem to be of significance in their own right (e.g. on 2400).

---

[12] In the bibliography 'Plates' prefaces all references to plates.

[13] Those whose interest is in miniatures should consult A. M. Friend Jr., 'The Portraits of the Evangelists in Greek and Latin Manuscripts', *Art Studies* 5 (Cambridge, Mass., 1927), 115–47 plus 184 illustrations; and 7 (1929), 3–29 plus 40 illustrations.

That comparatively little has been published on the lectionaries may be seen by examining the size of this section of the bibliography. Some background information on the lectionary text may be obtained from:

> E. C. Colwell and D. W. Riddle, *Prolegomena to the Study of the Lectionary Text of the Gospels* (Chicago, 1933);
>
> K. Junack, 'Zu den griechischen Lektionaren und ihrer Überlieferung der katholischen Briefe', in K. Aland (ed.), *Die Alten Übersetzungen des Neuen Testaments, die Kirchenväterzitante und Lektionare, Arbeiten zur Neutestamentlichen Textforschung* V (Berlin/New York, 1972), 498–593; and
>
> B. M. Metzger, 'Greek Lectionaries in a Critical Edition of the Greek New Testament', in ibid., 479–97.

See also J. Duplacy, 'Les Lectionnaires et l'édition du Nouveau Testament grec', in A. de Halleux (ed.), *Mélanges bibliques en hommage au R. P. Béda Rigaux* (Gembloux, 1970), 509–45. Reprinted in J. Delobel (ed.), *Études de critique textuelle du Nouveau Testament, Bibliotheca ephemeridum theologicarum Lovaniensium* LXXVIII (Louvain, 1987), 81–117.

Many manuscripts, particularly lectionaries, were noted by G. Krodel, 'New Manuscripts of the Greek New Testament', *JBL* 91 (1972), 232–8; not all of these have been published in the official *Liste*. Similarly not all the manuscripts identified by J. Noret, 'Manuscrits grecs du Nouveau Testament', *Anal Boll* 87 (1969), 460–9 have yet been accepted into the official list: many of these are lectionaries. See also J. N. Birdsall, 'Two Lectionaries in Birmingham, *JTS* XXXV (1984), 448–54.

By comparison with the lectionaries (and cursives), work on the papyri is extensive and relatively well covered in existing bibliographical tools that are easily accessible, such as:

> K. Aland (ed.), *Repertorium der griechischen christlichen Papyri* I, *Biblische Papyri, Patristische Texte und Studien* 18 (Berlin/New York, 1976):
>
> J. van Haelst, *Catalogue des papyrus littéraires juifs et chrétiens, Papyrologie* I (Paris, 1976).

T. C. Skeat in his major review of these books in *JTS* 29 (1970), 175–86 castigates Aland's bibliography for being over-inflated with ephemeral and unimportant references. Despite this criticism, there seemed no point in my compiling a separate full bibliography of works on the papyri: Aland (and van Haelst) are fairly up-to-date and reliable and there is no need to duplicate material in these sources. Thus, for the papyri, I have merely included details about the *editio princeps* and significant plates. Material absent from or incorrect in Aland and van Haelst has been given. As with other sections in my bibliography, general works have been ignored for the specific manuscripts, but the following may be of interest:

> P. Hedley, 'The Egyptian Text of the Gospels and Acts', *Church Quarterly Review* 118 (London, 1934), 23–39, 118–230 (describes the character of Egyptian manuscripts including Papyri 1, 5, 6, 19, 21, 36, 41, 44, 45);
> E. M. Schofield, *The Papyrus Fragments of the Greek New Testament*, unpublished Ph.D. thesis, Southern Baptist Theological Seminary, Louisville, Ky, 1936 (discussion, often with text, of Papyri 1–48);
> G. Milligan, *Here and There among the Papyri* (London, 1922).

Inevitably, some references that ought to have been included in this bibliography may have been overlooked. Similarly, some inconsistencies in presentation may become apparent: these blemishes are inevitable in a work that has been compiled from many different sources over several years. *Addenda* and *corrigenda* of this sort will be gratefully received by the author and it may well be that additional material, especially of newly published matter, can be published as occasional supplements to the present work in a learned journal.

Bibliographical material on textual criticism in general as well as on individual manuscripts may be found in:

> B. M. Metzger, *Annotated Bibliography of the Textual Criticism of the New Testament, Studies and Documents* 16 (Copenhagen, 1955);
> J. Duplacy, 'Bulletin de critique textuelle du Nouveau Testament':[14]

---

[14] See also J. Duplacy, *Où en est la critique textuelle du Nouveau Testament?* (Paris, 1959), which includes articles that originally appeared in *RSR* 45 (1957), 419–41 and *RSR* 46 (1958), 270–313, 431–62.

I *RSR* 50 (1962), 242–63
564–98
*RSR* 51 (1963), 432–62
II *RSR* 53 (1965), 257–84
*RSR* 54 (1966), 426–76

and (with C.M. Martini):

III *Biblica* 49 (1968), 515–51
*Biblica* 51 (1970), 84–129
IV *Biblica* 52 (1971), 79–113
*Biblica* 53 (1972), 245–78
V *Biblica* 54 (1973), 79–114
*Biblica* 58 (1977), 259–70, 542–68.

The appropriate sections in the following series may also be consulted with profit:

*Elenchus bibliographicus biblicus* (Rome, 1920–   );
*Internationale Zeitschriftenschau für Bibelwissenschaft und Grenzgebiete* (Stuttgart, 1951–   );

and in the journal:

*New Testament Abstracts* (Weston, Mass., 1956–   )

as well as in:

P.-E. Langevin, *Biblical Bibliography*, 2 vols. (Quebec, 1972 and 1978):
*L'Année philologique* (Paris, 1924–   );
*Revue d'histoire ecclésiastique* (Louvain, 1900–   ).

# PAPYRI

| | |
|---|---|
| P¹ | B.P. Grenfell and A.S. Hunt, *OP* I, pp. 4–7 and 1 plate |
| | Text repeated in Wessely, *Patr or* IV (1907), pp. 142 ff. and 1 plate |
| | J. O'Callaghan, *Stud pap* 10 (1971), 87–92 (on fragment containing Matt. 2.14) |
| | Clark, *USA*, pp. 341–2 |
| Plates | Sitterly (1914), II |
| | Hatch XI |
| | von Dobschütz I |
| P² | E. Pistelli, 'Papiri evangelici', *Rivista di studi religiosi* 6 (Florence, 1906), 129–40 and plates (see also Naldini, *Documenti*, no. 13, plate) |
| P³ | C. Wessely, 'Evangelien-Fragmente auf Papyrus', *Wien Stud* 4 (1882), 198–223 and 7 (1885), 69 f. (see also J.N. Birdsall, 'A Further Decipherment of Papyrus Gr 2323 ...', *Wien Stud* 76 (1963), 163–4) |
| P⁴ | F.V. Scheil, *Rev bib* I (1892), 113–15 |
| | Text (with commentary) in M.-J. Lagrange, *Critique textuelle* II, *La Critique rationelle* (Paris, 1935), pp. 118–23 |
| | J. Merell, *Rev bib* XLVII (1938), 5–22 and facsimiles (plates 1–7) |
| P⁵ | B.P. Grenfell and A.S. Hunt, *OP* II, pp. 1 ff. and *OP* XV, pp. 8–12 |
| | Text repeated in Wessely, *Patr or* IV (1907), pp. 145 ff. and XVIII (1924), pp. 499 ff. |
| Plates | Hatch VIII |
| P⁶ | F. Rösch, *Bruchstücke des ersten Clemensbriefes nach dem achmimischen Papyrus der Strassburger Universitäts- und Landesbibliothek* (Strasburg, 1910), pp. 119–60 |
| P⁷ | K. Aland, 'Neue Neutestamentliche Papyri', *NTS* 3 (1956–7), 261–86, esp. 262–5 |
| P⁸ | Gregory, *Textkritik* III (Leipzig, 1909), pp. 1086–90 |
| P⁹ | B.P. Grenfell and A.S. Hunt, *OP* III, pp. 2–3 |

|  | Clark, *USA*, pp. 117–18 |
|--|--|
|  | *ANTF* 6 |
| P[10] | B. P. Grenfell and A. S. Hunt, *OP* II, pp. 8–9 and 1 plate |
|  | Text repeated by W. C. Winslow, *Biblica* 14 (1901), 21 and plate |
|  | Text repeated in Wessely, *Patr or* IV (1907), pp. 148–50 (text) and plate II 8 |
|  | Clark, *USA*, pp. 115–16 |
| Plates | C. Wessely, *RGG* I, plate 6 |
|  | von Dobschütz II |
| P[11] | Schofield, pp. 141–51 |
|  | Treu, pp. 107–9 (see also Treu, *Fo und Fo* 13 (1957), 185–9 and plate) |
|  | K. Aland, 'Neue Neutestamentliche Papyri', *NTS* 3 (1956–7), 261–86, esp. 269–78 and 286 |
| P[12] | B. P. Grenfell and A. S. Hunt, *The Amherst Papyri* I 3[B] and 1 plate (London, 1900), pp. 28–31, and plate XXV in II (London, 1901) |
|  | Text repeated in Wessely, *Patr or* IV (1907), p. 138 |
|  | Clark, *USA*, pp. 170–1 |
| P[13] | B. P. Grenfell and A. S. Hunt, *OP* IV, pp. 36–48 |
|  | The Florence portion edited by V. Bartoletti and M. Norsa, *PSI* XII (1951), 209–10 |
| Plates | Vogels 2 |
|  | New Pal Soc I, 47 |
| P[14] | J. R. Harris, *Biblical Fragments from Mount Sinai* (London, 1890), pp. xiii, 54–6 (see also Treu, *Fo und Fo* 13 (1957), 185–9 and plate) |
| P[15] | B. P. Grenfell and A. S. Hunt, *OP* VII, pp. 4–8 |
|  | Text repeated in Wessely, *Patr or* XVIII (1924), pp. 457–60 |
| P[16] | B. P. Grenfell and A. S. Hunt, *OP* VII, pp. 8–11 |
|  | Text repeated in Wessely, *Patr or* XVIII (1924), pp. 460f. |

P[17]  B.P. Grenfell and A.S. Hunt, *OP* VIII, pp. 11–13
Text repeated in Wessely, *Patr or* XVIII (1924),
pp. 461 ff.

P[18]  B.P. Grenfell and A.S. Hunt, *OP* VIII, pp. 13–14
Text repeated in Wessely, *Patr or* XVIII (1924),
pp. 465 ff.
Text repeated in R.H. Charles, *Revelation of St
John, ICC*, vol. II (Edinburgh, 1920), pp. 447–9

P[19]  B.P. Grenfell and A.S. Hunt, *OP* IX, pp. 7–9

P[20]  B.P. Grenfell and A.S. Hunt, *OP* IX, pp. 9–11
and plate I
Text repeated in Wessely, *Patr or* XVIII (1924),
pp. 464–5

Clark, *USA*, pp. 181–2

M.-J. Lagrange, *Critique textuelle* II, *La Critique
rationelle* (Paris, 1935), pp. 533–4

*ANTF*, 6

Plates  Hatch VI

P[21]  B.P. Grenfell and A.S. Hunt, *OP* X, pp. 12–14

Clark, *USA*, p. 139

P[22]  B.P. Grenfell and A.S. Hunt, *OP* X, pp. 14–16
Text repeated in Wessely, *Patr or* XVIII,
pp. 451–2

Plates  G. Milligan, *The New Testament and its Transmission* (London, 1932), plate 1

Hatch VII

P[23]  B.P. Grenfell and A.S. Hunt, *OP* X, pp. 16–18
Text repeated in Wessely, *Patr or* XVIII, pp. 463–4

*ANTF* 6

Clark, *USA*, p. 274

M.-J. Lagrange, *Critique textuelle* II, *La Critique
rationelle* (Paris, 1935), p. 534

P[24]  B.P. Grenfell and A.S. Hunt, *OP* X, pp. 18–19
Text repeated in Wessely, *Patr or* XVIII (1924),
p. 467
Text repeated in R.H. Charles, *Revelation of St
John, ICC*, vol. II (Edinburgh, 1920), pp. 448–50

|  | Clark, *USA*, p. 5 |
| $P^{25}$ | O. Stegmüller, 'Ein Bruchstück aus dem griechischen Diatessaron', *ZNW* 37 (1938), 223–9 |
|  | Clark, *USA*, p. 79 |
| $P^{26}$ | B. P. Grenfell and A. S. Hunt, *OP* XI, pp. 6–9 |
|  | Clark, *USA*, p. 212 |
| $P^{27}$ | B. P. Grenfell and A. S. Hunt, *OP* XI, pp. 9–12 and plate I<br>Text repeated in Wessely, *Patr or* XVIII, pp. 455f. |
| Plates | Hatch IX |
| $P^{28}$ | B. P. Grenfell and A. S. Hunt, *OP* XIII, pp. 8–10 |
|  | Clark, *USA*, p. 148 |
| Plates | Finegan 10 |
| $P^{29}$ | B. P. Grenfell and A. S. Hunt, *OP* XIII, pp. 10–12 and plate I |
|  | J. H. Ropes, *Beginnings of Christianity* III, pp. xvii, ccxff., 235, 237 (text and collation) |
| $P^{30}$ | B. P. Grenfell and A. S. Hunt, *OP* XIII, pp. 12–14 |
| Plates | Wittek 13 |
|  | Hatch V |
| $P^{31}$ | A. S. Hunt, *Catalogue of the Greek Papyri in the John Rylands Library* (Manchester/London, 1911–15), I, pp. 9f. |
| Plates | Hatch III |
| $P^{32}$ | A. S. Hunt, *Catalogue of the Greek Papyri in the John Rylands Library* (London/Manchester, 1911–15), I, pp. 10–11 |
| $P^{33}$ | C. Wessely, *Stud zur Pal und Pap* XII (Leipzig, 1912), p. 245<br>(See also $P^{58}$) |
| $P^{34}$ | C. Wessely, *Stud zur Pal und Pap* XII (Leipzig, 1912), p. 246 |
| $P^{35}$ | E. Pistelli, *PSI* I (1912), pp. 1–2<br>(see also Naldini, *Documenti*, no. 10 and plate) |
| $P^{36}$ | E. Pistelli, *PSI* I (1912), pp. 5–6 (see also Naldini, *Documenti*, no. 14 and plate) |

Extra material in A. Carlini, *APF* 22/23 (1974), 219–22; see also id., *Papiri litterari greci* 28 (Pisa, 1978), 193–9

G. H. R. Horsley, 'Scribal Carelessness in P$^{36}$?', in *New Documents Illustrating Early Christianity*, 3 (Macquarie University, 1983), pp. 100–1

**P$^{37}$**

Henry A. Sanders, 'An Early Papyrus Fragment of the Gospel of Matthew in the Michigan Collection', *HTR* XIX (1926), 215–26 (transcription, collation, facsimile)

Henry A. Sanders, *Michigan Papyri, University of Michigan Studies*, Humanistic Series, XL (Ann Arbor, 1936), pp. 9–14 (transcription) (see also J.-M. Bover, *EE* 9 (1930), 289–330)

Clark, *USA*, pp. 334–5

**Plates** Hatch XIII

**P$^{38}$**

Henry A. Sanders, 'A Papyrus Fragment of Acts in the Michigan Collection', *HTR* XX (1927), 1–19 (transcription, collation, facsimile)

A. C. Clark, 'The Michigan Fragment of Acts', *JTS* XXIX (1927), 18–28

M.-J. Lagrange, 'Un nouveau papyrus contenant un fragment des Actes', *Rev bib* XXXVI (1927), 549–60 (text)

Text (correcting Sanders), in A. C. Clark, *Acts of the Apostles* (Oxford, 1933), pp. 220–5

Silva New, 'The Michigan Papyrus Fragment 1571', *Beginnings of Christianity* V (1933), pp. 262–8 (text and plate)

M.-J. Lagrange, *Critique textuelle* II, *La Critique rationelle* (Paris, 1935), pp. 402–5 (transcription)

Henry A. Sanders, *Michigan Papyri, University of Michigan Studies*, Humanistic Series, XL (Ann Arbor, 1936), pp. 14–19 (transcription)

Clark, *USA*, pp. 335–6

**Plates** Vogels 1

**P$^{39}$**

B. P. Grenfell and A. S. Hunt, *OP* XV, pp. 7–8

Clark, *USA*, p. 29

P⁴⁰ Text (incomplete), in F. Bilabel, *Veröffentlichungen aus den Badischen Papyrussammlungen* IV (Heidelberg, 1924), pp. 28–31 and pp. 124–7

P⁴¹ Text set out in full in appendix I of J. H. Ropes, *Beginnings of Christianity* III, pp. xxi, ccxi, 271–5

C. Wessely, *Stud zur Pal und Pap* XV (Leipzig, 1914), pp. 107–18
New edition by P. Weigandt, *ANTF* 3, pp. 54–72 (and see also 0236)

F.-J. Schmitz, 'Neue Fragmente zum P⁴¹', *Bericht der Hermann Kunst-stiftung zur Förderung der neutestamentlichen Textforschung für die Jahre 1985 bis 1987* (Münster, 1988), pp. 78–97

P⁴² P. Sanz and W. Till, 'Eine griechisch-koptische Odenhandschrift', in *Monumenta biblica et ecclesiastica* V (Rome, 1939), pp. 9–112 and plate (see also *editio princeps* of one page in Wessely, *Stud zur Pal und Pap* IX (1909), no. 3)

P⁴³ W. E. Crum and H. I. Bell, *Coptica* III, *Wadi Sarga: Coptic and Greek Texts from the Excavations Undertaken by the Byzantine Research Account* (Copenhagen, 1922), pp. 43–51

P⁴⁴ W. E. Crum and H. G. Evelyn-White, *The Monastery of Epiphanius at Thebes, Metropolitan Museum of Art, Egyptian Expedition Publications* IV (New York, 1926), II, pp. 120–1 (transcription and collation) and plate

Clark, *USA*, pp. 135–6

P⁴⁵ F. G. Kenyon, *The Chester Beatty Biblical Papyri* II (London: text (1933); plates (1934))

Vienna fragment in Hans Gerstinger, 'Ein Fragment des Chester Beatty-Evangelienkodex in der Papyrussammlung der Nationalbibliothek in Wien', *Aegyptus* XIII (1933), 67–72

G. Zuntz, 'Reconstruction of one leaf of the Chester Beatty Papyri of the Gospels and Acts', *Chronique d'Égypte* 26 (Brussels, 1951), 191–211

M.-J. Lagrange, *Critique textuelle* II, *La Critique rationelle* (Paris, 1935), pp. 158–63, 413–16

C. A. Phillips, 'The Caesarean Text with special reference to the new Papyrus and another Ally', *BBC* 10 (1932), 5–19

(See P[75]: Birdsall)

Plates     A & A 30

Seider II, pp. 118–20 and plate XXI

Hatch IV

Kenyon–Adams, *Our Bible*, XX

P[46]     H. A. Sanders, *A Third Century Papyrus Codex of the Epistles of Paul, University of Michigan Studies*, Humanistic Series, XXXVIII (Ann Arbor, 1935) and plates

F. G. Kenyon, *The Chester Beatty Biblical Papyri* III, Supplement (London: text (1936); plates (1937)); see also III (London 1934, 1936)

H. C. Hoskier, 'A Study of the Chester Beatty Codex of the Pauline Epistles', *JTS* XXXVIII (1937), 148–63

S. Giversen, 'The Pauline Epistles on Papyrus', in *Die Paulinische Literatur und Theologie*, ed. Sigfred Pedersen (Göttingen, 1980), pp. 201–12

Y. K. Kim, 'Palaeographical Dating of P[46] to the later First Century, *Biblica* 69 (1988), 248–57

M.-J. Lagrange, *Critique textuelle* II, *La Critique rationelle* (Paris, 1935), pp. 473–5

Clark, *USA*, pp. 336–40

Plates     Hatch II

G. Milligan, *The New Testament and its Transmission* (London, 1932), pp. 191 f.

Kenyon–Adams, *Our Bible*, XXI

Clark, *USA*, frontispiece

A & A 25

Metzger, *Manuscripts*, 6

Metzger, *Text*, 2

P[47]     F. G. Kenyon, *The Chester Beatty Biblical Papyri* III (London: text (1934); plates (1936))

| | |
|---|---|
| Plates | Hatch X |
| | A & A 27 |
| P[48] | G. Vitelli and G. Mercati, *PSI* X (1932), 112–18 (see also Naldini, *Documenti*, no. 15 and plate, and A. C. Clark, *The Acts of the Apostles* (Oxford, 1933), pp. 409–13) |
| | M.-J. Lagrange, *Critique textuelle* II, *La Critique rationelle* (Paris, 1935), pp. 401–9 (transcription) |
| Plates | A & A 17 |
| | Hatch XII |
| P[49] | W. H. P. Hatch and C. B. Welles, 'A Hitherto Unpublished Fragment of the Epistle to the Ephesians', *HTR* LI (1958), 33–7 and plate |
| | Clark, *USA*, p. 374 |
| P[50] | C. H. Kraeling, 'Two Selections from Acts', in Lake F/S, pp. 163–72 and plate |
| | Clark, *USA*, p. 374 |
| P[51] | E. Lobel, C. H. Roberts, and E. P. Wegener, *OP* XVIII, pp. 1–3, 8 |
| | Schofield, 330–4 (not in Aland, *Repertorium*) |
| P[52] | C. H. Roberts, *An Unpublished Fragment of the Fourth Gospel in the John Rylands Library* (Manchester, 1935), and plate; republished, with slight alterations, in *BJRL*, XX (1936), 44–55, and again, with bibliography of reviews and opinions expressed by other scholars, in C. H. Roberts, *Catalogue of the Greek and Latin Papyri in the John Rylands Library*, III (Manchester, 1938), pp. 1–3 |
| Plates | Hatch I |
| | Kenyon–Adams, *Our Bible*, XXII |
| | A & A 23 |
| | Finegan 3 |
| | Metzger, *Manuscripts*, 4 |
| P[53] | H. A. Sanders, 'A Third Century Papyrus of Matthew and Acts', in Lake F/S, pp. 151–61, and plate |

Clark, *USA*, p. 340

P $^{54}$  H. Kase, *Papyri in the Princeton University Collections*, II (Princeton, 1936), pp. 1−3

*ANTF* 6

P $^{55}$  P. Sanz, *Mitteilungen aus der Papyrussammlung der österreichischen Nationbibliothek in Wien*, N.S., IV (Baden, 1946), pp. 58−9

P $^{56}$  See Sanz (for P $^{55}$), pp. 65−6

P $^{57}$  See Sanz (for P $^{55}$), pp. 66−7

P $^{58}$  See Sanz (for P $^{55}$), pp. 67 f.

(P $^{58}$ = P $^{33}$)  See K. Aland, 'Neue Neutestamentliche Papyri II', *Nov T* 9 (1962−3), 306−16

P $^{59}$  L. Casson and E. L. Hettich, *Excavations at Nessana* II, *Literary Papyri* (Princeton, 1950), pp. 79−122 and plate

P $^{60}$  See Casson and Hettich (P $^{59}$) and plate

Plates  Finegan 6 and 7

P $^{61}$  See Casson and Hettich (P $^{59}$) and plate

P $^{62}$  L. Amundsen, 'Christian Papyri from the Oslo Collection', *Symbolae Osloenses* 24 (Oslo, 1945), 121−47

P $^{63}$  O. Stegmüller, 'Zu den Bibelorakeln im Codex Bezae', *Biblica* 34 (1953), 13−22

P $^{64}$  (see also P $^{67}$) C. H. Roberts, 'An Early Papyrus of the First Gospel', *HTR* XLVI (1953), 233−7 and plate

P $^{65}$  V. Bartolotti, *PSI* XIV (1957), pp. 5−7 (see also Naldini, *Documenti*, no. 17 and plate)

P $^{66}$  V. Martin, *Papyrus Bodmer* II, *Évangile de Jean*, chaps. 1−14 (Cologny−Geneva, 1956); id., *Supplément*, chaps. 14−21 (1958)

A new edition of the *Supplément*, augmented and corrected, was published in 1962 with the assistance of J. W. B. Barns, accompanied by a photographic reproduction of the entire manuscript (chaps. i−xxi). For still further emendations see J. W. B. Barns, 'Papyrus Bodmer II, Some

Corrections and Remarks', *Muséon* LXXV (1962), 327–9.[1]

J.N. Birdsall, *The Bodmer Papyrus of the Gospel of John* (London, 1960)

G.D. Fee, 'The Corrections of Papyrus Bodmer II', *Nov T* 7 (1965), 247–57

G.D. Fee, *Papyrus Bodmer II (P$^{66}$): its Textual Relationships and Scribal Characteristics*, *S & D* 34 (Salt Lake City, 1968), appendix A – an annotated list of corrections to the *editio princeps*

M. Gronewald in *Papyrologica Coloniensia*, Sonderreihe VII, *Kölner Papyri*, no.5, ed. M. Gronewald *et al. Abhandlungen der Rheinisch-Westfälischen Akademie der Wissenschaften* (Cologne, 1985), pp.73–6

Plates A & A 26

Metzger, *Manuscripts*, 7

Seider II, pp.121–2 and plate XXII

Finegan 4, 5, 8, 11, and 12

P$^{67}$ (see P$^{64}$)

R. Roca-Puig, *Un papiro griego del Evangelio de San Mateo* (Sabadell, 1956; 2nd. edn., with a note by C.H. Roberts, Barcelona, 1962) and plates (see also id., *Helmantica*, 37 (1961), 103–24)

K. Aland, 'Neue Neutestamentliche Papyri', *NTS* 3 (1956–7), 261–86, esp. 279ff. and 9 (1962–3), 303–16

P$^{68}$ K. Aland, 'Neue Neutestamentliche Papyri', *NTS* 3 (1956–7), 261–86, esp. 265–9

---

[1] For further studies of P$^{66}$ see M.E. Boismard in *Rev bib* LXX (1963), 120–33; Miguel Balgue in *Stud pap* IV (1965), 76–89; E.C. Colwell, 'Scribal Habits in Early Papyri: a Study in the Corruption of the Text', in *The Bible in Modern Scholarship*, ed. J. Philip Hyatt (Nashville, 1965), pp.370–89; E.F. Rhodes, 'The Corrections of Papyrus Bodmer II', *NTS* 14 (1967–8), 271–81; K. Aland, 'Neue Neutestamentliche Papyri', *NTS* 3 (1956–7), 261–86, esp.279–84; 20 (1974), 357–81; J.B. Bauer, 'Zur Datierung des Papyrus Bodmer II (P$^{66}$)', *TZ* 24 (1968), 121–2.

Treu, p. 109

P[69]   E. Lobel, C.H. Roberts, E.G. Turner, and J.W.B. Barns, *OP* XXIV, pp. 1–4 and plate XIII

K. Aland, 'Alter und Entstehung des D-Textes in Neuen Testament. Betrachtungen zu P[69] und 0171', in *Miscel-lànea papirològica Ramon Roca-Puig*, ed. S. Janeras (Barcelona, 1987), pp. 37–61

P[70]   E. Lobel, C.H. Roberts, E.G. Turner, and J.W.B. Barns, *OP* XXIV, pp. 4–5, and 1 plate

Extra portion edited by M. Naldini, 'Nuovi Frammenti del Vangelo di Matteo', *Prometheus* 1 (Florence, 1975), 195–200 and 1 plate

P[71]   E. Lobel, C.H. Roberts, E.G. Turner, and J.W.B. Barns, *OP* XXIV, pp. 5–6 and 1 plate

P[72]   M. Testuz, *Papyrus Bodmer VII-IX* (Cologny–Geneva, 1959) and 2 plates

Facsimile edition by C.M. Martini, *Beati Petri Apostoli Epistulae, Ex Papyro Bodmeriana VIII* (Milan, 1968)

F.W. Beare, 'The Text of I Peter in the Bodmer Papyrus (P[72])', in *Studia evangelica* III, ed. F.L. Cross, *T & U* LXXXVIII (Berlin, 1964), pp. 263–5

E. Massaux, 'Le Texte de l'Épître de Jude du Papyrus Bodmer VII', in *Scrinium Lovaniense: Mélanges historiques Étienne Van Cauwenberg* (Louvain, 1961), pp. 108–25

J.N. Birdsall, 'The Text of Jude in P[72]', *JTS* XIV (1963), pp. 394–9

*ANTF* 6

Plates   A & A 29

P[73]   K. Aland, 'Neue Neutestamentliche Papyri II', *NTS* 9 (1962–3), 303–16, esp. 303, 308

P[74]   R. Kasser, *Papyrus Bodmer XVII* (Cologny–Geneva, 1961)

*ANTF* 6

Plates   A & A 24

P[75]    V. Martin and R. Kasser, *Papyrus Bodmer* XIV-XV (Cologny–Geneva, 1961)

C.L. Porter, 'Papyrus Bodmer XV and The Text of Codex Vaticanus', *JBL* LXXX (1962), 363–76

C.L. Porter, 'An Analysis of the Textual Variations between Pap 75 and Codex Vaticanus in the Text of John', in Clark F/S, pp. 71–80

M. Mees, 'Papyrus Bodmer XIV (P[75]) und die Lukaszitate bei Clemens von Alexandrien', *Lateranum* 34 (Rome, 1968), 97–120

J. Duplacy, 'P[75] et les formes les plus anciennes du texte de *Luc*', in *Évangile de Luc*, ed. F. Nierynck (Gembloux, 1973), pp. 111–12

S.A. Edwards, 'P[75] under the Magnifying Glass', *Nov T* 18 (1976), 190–212

J.N. Birdsall, 'Rational Criticism and the Oldest Manuscripts: A Comparative Study of the Bodmer and Chester Beatty Papyri of the Gospel of Luke, in *Studies in New Testament Language and Text*, ed. J.K. Elliott, *Supplements to Novum Testamentum* XLIV (Leiden, 1976), pp. 39–51

K. Aland, 'Neue Neutestamentliche Papyri III', *NTS* 22 (1976), 375–96

Plates    A & A 28

Finegan 9, 13, and 14

Seider II, pp. 132–3 and plate XXV

Metzger, *Text*, 3

Metzger, *Manuscripts* 9

P[76]    H. Hunger, 'Zwei unbekannte neutestamentliche Papyrusfragmente der österreichischen Nationalbibliothek', *Biblos* VIII (Vienna, 1959), 7–12 and plate p. 5, and XIX (1970), 71–5

Plates    Cavallo 105

P[77]    L. Ingrams, P. Kingston, P.J. Parsons, and J.R. Rea, *OP* XXXIV, pp. 1–3 and 2 plates

P[78]    L. Ingrams, P. Kingston, P.J. Parsons, and J.R. Rea, *OP* XXXIV, pp. 4–6 and 2 plates

$P^{78}$  M. Mees, '$P^{78}$: ein neuer Textzeuge für den Judasbrief', *Orient Press* I (Rome, 1970), pp. 5–10

*ANTF* 6

$P^{79}$  Treu, *APF* 18 (1966), 37–48 and plate IV

M. Mees, 'Einige Verse aus den Hebräerbrief nach einem neugefundeten Papyrus', *Orient Press* I (Rome 1970), pp. 43–6

Horsley, pp. 125–40

$P^{80}$  R. Roca-Puig, 'Papior del Evangelio de San Juan con "Hermeneia"', in *Atti dell XI Congresso Internazionale di Papirologia* (Milan, 1966), pp. 225–36 and plates

$P^{81}$  S. Daris, 'Uno nuovo frammento della prima lettera di Pietro', in *Papyrologica Castroctaviana, Studia et Textus* 2 (Barcelona, 1967), pp. 11–37 and 2 plates

*ANTF* 6

$P^{82}$  J. Schwartz, 'Fragment d'évangile sur papyrus', *ZPE* 3 (1968), 157–8

$P^{85}$  J. Schwartz, 'Papyrus et tradition manuscrite', *ZPE* 4 (1969), 178, 181 f.

$P^{86}$  C. Charalambakis, D. Hagedorn, D. Kaimakis, and L. Thüngen, 'Vier literarische Papyri der Kölner Sammlung', no. 4, *ZPE* 14 (1974), 37–40 and plate $II^c$

B. Kramer and D. Hagedorn, *Papyrologica Coloniensia* VII, 2 (Cologne, 1978), pp. 88–9

$P^{87}$  C. Römer, *Papyrologica Coloniensia* VII, 4 (Cologne, 1984), 28–31 and plate 1b

$P^{88}$  S. Daris, *Aegyptus* 52 (1972) 80–8, and plate

$P^{89}$  R. Pintaudi, *ZPE* 42 (1981), 42–4 and plates Id and Ie (reprinted in *Papyrologica Florentina* 12 (Florence, 1983), pp. 37 f.)

$P^{90}$  T. C. Skeat, *OP* 50, pp. 3–8 and 1 plate

$P^{91}$  C. Gallazzi, 'P. Mil. Vogl. Inv. 1224: Novum Testamentum, Act, 2.30–7 e 2,46–3.2', *Bulletin of the American Society of Papyrologists* 19 (New Haven, Conn., 1982), 39–43 and reproduction

S. R. Pickering, *ZPE* 65 (1986), pp. 76−8 and 2 plates (see also Treu, *APF* 31 (1985), 61)

P[92]     C. Gallazzi, 'Frammenti di un Codice con le epistole di Paolo', *ZPE* 46 (1982), 117−22

P[93]     G. Bastianini, 'Trenta testi greci da Papiri letterari e documentari, a cura di M Manfredi', no. 4 (Florence, 1983), pp. 10−11 ( = *Proceedings of the XVII Congresso Internationale di Papirologia* (Naples, 1983) and 1 plate

P[94]     C. Bingen, 'P[94]: Épître aux Romains 6, 10−13, 19−22 (P. Cair 10730)', in *Miscel-lània papirològica Ramon Roca-Puig*, ed. S. Janeras (Barcelona, 1987), pp. 75−8 and plates

P[95]     J. Lenaerts, 'Un papyrus de l'évangile de Jean PL II/31', *Chronique d'Egypte* LX (Brussels, 1985), 117−20 and plate

# UNCIALS

01 ℵ Text reproduced as quasi-facsimile by C.
Tischendorf, *Codex Sinaiticus Petropolitanus*, 4
vols. (N.T. = vol. 4) (Leipzig, 1862; reprinted
Hildersheim, 1969); two further fragments in id.,
*Appendix codicum celeberrimorum Sinaitici
Vaticani Alexandrini* (Leipzig, 1867), pp. 3–6;
additional fragment ed. H. Brugsch (Leipzig, 1875).
The New Testament part was published separately
in a critical edition by C. Tischendorf, *Novum
Testamentum Sinaiticum cum epistola Barnabae et
fragmentis Pastoris, etc.* (Leipzig, 1863), and, in a
more popular form, *Novum Testamentum Graece
ex Sinaitico codice omnium antiquissimo* (Leipzig,
1865) (see also C. Tischendorf, *Die Sinaibibel: Ihre
Entdeckung, Herausgabe, und Erwerbung* (Leipzig,
1871). Photographic edition: *Codex Sinaiticus
Petropolitanus* by H. and K. Lake (2 vols., Oxford,
1911–22), with introduction by K. Lake.

F. H. A. Scrivener, *A Full Collation of the Codex
Sinaiticus*, 2nd edn. (Cambridge, 1867) (see also
Hansell III, app. I). (Both collate against the *textus
receptus* of 1550.)

Selection of general background books and articles
on the Codex Sinaiticus:

Heinrich Ewald, *Göttingische Gelehrte Anzeigen*
(1860), pp. 1761–8, and (1868), pp. 1378–92

Abraham Kuenen, *Algemeene Konst- en Letterbode*
(1860), nr 2 and 14; cf. ibid. (9 February 1861),
pp. 41–4 (see also id., *Teekenen des Tijds*, vol. 1,
nr 32)

A. P. Buttmann, *Theologische Studien und Kritiken*
(Hamburg, 1860), pp. 730–8

Carl Wieseler, *Theologische Studien und Kritiken*
(Hamburg, 1861), pp. 790–803–10

A. P. Buttmann, *Zeitschrift für das Gymnasialwesen*
XV (Berlin, 1861), 123–9

A. Dutau, *Études de théologie* 3 (Paris, 1861),
660–75

A.P. Buttmann, *Zeitschrift für wissenschaftliche Theologie* (Leipzig, 1864), 367–92

A. Hilgenfeld, *Zeitschrift für wissenschaftliche Theologie* (Leipzig, 1864), 74–82 and 211–19; see also Tischendorf's reply in *Zeitschrift für wissenschaftliche Theologie* (Leipzig, 1864), 202–10, and in *Appendix codicum celeberrimorum* (Leipzig, 1867), p. viii.

J.W. Burgon, *The Last Twelve Verses of the Gospel according to S. Mark* (London, 1871), pp. 291–4: 'On the relative antiquity of the codex Vaticanus (B) and the codex Sinaiticus (א)'.

Ezra Abbot, 'On the Comparative Antiquity of the Sinaitic and Vatican Manuscripts of the Greek Bible', *Journal of the American Oriental Society* (Baltimore, 1872) vol. X no. 1, 189 ff.

A. Gardthausen, *Griechische Paläographie* (Leipzig, 1879), pp. 143–50 and 2nd ed (Leipzig, 1911–13), vol. 2, pp. 119–34

Charles A. Hay, 'Peculiarities of the Codex Sinaiticus', *The Lutheran Quarterly* (Gettysburg, Pennsylvania, 1880), 153–75

B.F. Westcott and F.J.A. Hort, *The New Testament in the Original Greek: Introduction* (London, 1881), pp. 210–30, 246–71

F.H.A. Scrivener, *A Plain Introduction to the Criticism of the New Testament* I, ed. E. Miller, 4th edn. (London, 1894), pp. 90–7

F.G. Kenyon, *Our Bible and the Ancient Manuscripts* (London, 1895), pp. 121–8 (cf. 5th edn by A.W. Adams (London, 1958), pp. 119 f., 191–8 and plate XXIII)

H.S. Cronin, 'An Examination of some Omissions of the Codex Sinaiticus in St. John's Gospel', *JTS* XIII (1912), 563–71

M.-J. Lagrange, 'Le Manuscrit sinaitique', *Rev bib* 35 (1926), 89–93

Gregor Peradze, [*Documents which bear upon the Question of the Discovery and the Text of the Sinai Codex*] (Warsaw, 1934) (In Polish with a French résumé)

A. Lods, 'Le Codex Sinaiticus', *Revue archéologique*, Sixth Series, 2 (Paris, 1934), 263–4

A. J. Collins, 'The Codex Sinaiticus', *BMQ* 8 (1933/34), 89

A. Souter, 'The Codex Sinaiticus', *ET* 45 (1933/34), 335–6

[H. I. Bell], *The Mount Sinai Manuscript of the Bible* (published by the Trustees of The British Museum, 1934)

C. Tischendorf, *Codex Sinaiticus, the Ancient Biblical Manuscript now in the British Museum. Tischendorf's Story and Argument Related by himself* (London, 1934)

M.-J. Lagrange, *Critique Textuelle* II, *La Critique rationelle* (Paris, 1935), pp. 90–107

*Beginnings of Christianity* vol. III, pt 1, pp. xliv–l

H. J. M. Milne and T. C. Skeat, *Scribes and Correctors of the Codex Sinaiticus* (London, 1938); idd., *The Codex Sinaiticus and the Codex Alexandrinus* (London, 1951, 1963) and plates

A. Merk, 'Recentiora quaedam de codice Sinaitico', *Biblica* 19 (1938), 202–3 (data from Skeat and Milne's article in the *Daily Telegraph*, 11 and 12 January 1938, regarding their work on codex Sinaiticus)

C. A. Phillips, 'The Codex Sinaiticus and the Codex Alexandrinus', *ET* 51 (1939/40), 299–301

Christian Tindall, *Contributions to the Statistical Study of the Codex Sinaiticus*, ed. T. B. Smith (Edinburgh and London, 1961)

I. Ševčenco, 'New Documents on Constantine Tischendorf and the Codex Sinaiticus', *Scriptorium* XVIII (1964), 55–80

G.D. Fee, 'Codex Sinaiticus in the Gospel of John', *NTS* 15 (1968–9), 22–44

J.K. Elliott, *Codex Sinaiticus and the Simonides Affair, Analeka Vlatadon 33* (Thessalonica, 1982)

P. Magerson, 'Codex Sinaiticus: An Historical Observation', *Bib Arch* 46 (1983), 54–6

H.C. Hoskier, *Codex B and Its Allies, a Study and an Indictment* (London, 1914) (= 03 and 01)

Plates     Sitterly (1898), 3

Kenyon (1912), III

Pattie 11

Pal Soc, I, 105

Hatch XV and XVI

Milligan VII

von Dobschütz 6 and 7

Finegan 17

Metzger, *Text*, 4

A & A 7

Vogels 4

Cavallo 36, 37, 38

Plates*

02 A     The Codex Alexandrinus was one of the earliest of the uncial MSS to be made available to scholars. It was used by B. Walton in the *Biblia polyglotta* (6 vols., London, 1657). It was printed in facsimile by C.G. Woide, *NT Graecum e codice ms. alexandrino* (London, 1786),[1] and in ordinary type by B.H. Cowper, *Codex Alexandrinus* (London, 1860), who corrected some mistakes of Woide; and in photographic facsimile by the trustees of the British Museum, ed. E.M. Thompson (*Facsimile of the Codex Alexandrinus* (4 vols., London, 1879–83; NT = vol. IV)). Bentley's collation of 1675 of an edition of Fell's NT is to be found in Trinity

---

[1] See also C.G. Woide, *Notitia Codicis Alexandrini cum variis eius lectionibus omnibus* (London, 1788).

College Library, Cambridge. For a full description of the manuscript see E. M. Thompson's introduction to his photographic facsimile edition (London, 1879–83); a reduced photographic facsimile, with introduction by Frederic G. Kenyon, was published by the British Museum in 1909.

*Catalogue of Ancient Manuscripts in the British Museum* (London, 1881), pp. 17a–20a and plate 7

Hansell I and II (full text in parallel with other uncials)

*The Beginnings of Christianity* vol. III, pt I, pp. li–lv

H. J. M. Milne and T. C. Skeat, *Scribes and Correctors of the Codex Sinaiticus* (London, 1938), pp. 91 ff.; idd., *The Codex Sinaiticus and the Codex Alexandrinus* (London, 1951, 1963) and plates

F. C. Burkitt, 'Codex "Alexandrinus"', *JTS* XI (1909–10), 663–6

M.-J. Lagrange, *Critique textuelle* II, *La Critique rationelle* (Paris, 1935), pp. 83–9, 99–107, 125–41

Matthew Spinka, 'Acquisition of Codex Alexandrinus by England', *JR* 16 (1936), 20–9

S. Lake, *Family Π and the Codex Alexandrinus, the Text According to Mark*, *S & D* V (London, 1937)

J. Geerlings, 'Collation of Codex A with Family Π in Luke', in J. Geerlings, *Family Π in Luke*, *S & D* XXII (Salt Lake City, 1962), pp. 139–60

J. Geerlings, 'Collation of A with Family Π in John', in J. Geerlings, *Family Π in John*, *S & D* XXIII (Salt Lake City, 1963), pp. 101–11

'Collation of Codex Alexandrinus with Codex Π and the *Textus Receptus* in Matthew by R. Champlin' in R. Champlin, *Family Π in Mark*, *S & D* XXIV (Salt Lake City, 1964) pp. 151–63

T. C. Skeat, 'The Provenance of the Codex Alexandrinus', *JTS* VI (1955), 233–5

| Plates | Cavalieri and Lietzmann 1 |
|---|---|
| | Kenyon—Adams, *Our Bible*, XXIV |
| | Kenyon (1912) |
| | Kenyon, *Facsimiles*, II |
| | Pal Soc I, 106 |
| | von Dobschütz 6 and 7 |
| | Metzger, *Manuscripts*, 18 |
| | Finegan 21 |
| | Cavallo 63, 64, 65 |
| | Pattie 7 |
| | Vogels 6 |
| | A & A 3 |
| | Hatch XVII, XVIII, and XIX |
| | Sitterly (1898), 5 |
| Plates* | |
| (02: | see 041, S. Lake) |
| 03 B | The first collation of the manuscript, made in 1669, by Bartolocci, then librarian of the Vatican, exists only in manuscript in the Bibliothèque Nationale in Paris. Another was made by Birch, 1788–1801. The collation made for R. Bentley by an Italian named Mico was published by Ford, 1790. J.L. Hug wrote a learned *Commentatio de antiquitate codicis Vaticani* (Freiburg, 1810). The manuscript was then in Paris, but it was later restored to Rome, when it became practically inaccessible. An inaccurate and critically worthless edition of the whole manuscript was prepared by Cardinal Mai between 1828 and 1838.[2] C. Vercellone, J. Cozza, and G. Sergio published an edition of the entire codex in 6 vols. (New Testament is vol. V; VI = *Prolegomena*) in Rome, 1868–81; a typographical facsimile appeared between 1868 and 1872 and a photographic reproduction was published by the Vatican (1889) |

[2] Mai's edition was published posthumously (Rome, 1857); improved edn (Rome, 1859).

Ed. C. Tischendorf, *Nov. Test. Vaticanum* (Leipzig, 1867) and *Appendix N.T. Vatican* (Leipzig, 1869) For a photographic reproduction of the codex published by the authorities of the Vatican Library see *Bibliorum SS. Graecorum Codex Vaticanus 1209* (Milan, 1904–7) (see also J.H. Ropes in *Beginnings of Christianity* III, pt I, xxxiff. (text and *v. 11* for Acts))

In 1968 the New Testament portion was issued by the Vatican in photographic facsimile in colour (with an introduction by Carlo M. Martini) (see E. Tisserant, 'Notes sur le préparation de l'édition en fac-similé typographique du Codex Vaticanus (B)', *Angelicum* XX (1943), 237–48).

A. Rahlfs, 'Alter und Heimat der vaticanischen Bibelhandschrift', *Nachrichten der K. Gesellschaft der Wissenschaften zu Göttingen Phil-hist. Klasse* I (1899), pp. 72–9

L. Cerfaux, 'Problèmes autour du N.T.; 1, Le Problème du "Vaticanus"', *Collationes Dioecesis Tornacensis* 30 (Tournai, 1935), 373–83

M.-J. Lagrange, *Critique textuelle* II, *La Critique rationelle* (Paris, 1935), pp. 466–7

Hansell I, II, and III (appendix II 1)

S. Kubo, *P72 and the Codex Vaticanus, S & D* XXVII (Salt Lake City, 1965)

C.M. Martini, *Il problema della recensionalità del Codice B alla Luce del Papiro Bodmer* XIV (P75), *Analecta biblica*, 26 (Rome, 1966)

Janco Šagi, S.J., 'Problema historiae codicis B', *Divus Thomas commentarium de philosophia et theologica* lxxv (1972), pp. 3–29

T.C. Skeat, 'The Codex Vaticanus in the Fifth Century', *JTS* 35 (1984), 454–65

C.L. Porter, *JBL* LXXX (1962), 363–76, and id., Clark F/S, pp. 71–80 (see also P75)

Plates Kenyon–Adams, *Our Bible*, XXV

Sitterly (1898), 4

Kenyon (1912), V

Vogels, 3

Metzger, *Manuscripts*, 13

Cavalieri and Lietzmann 1

Hatch XIV

Finegan 15 and 16

Pal Soc I, 104

A & A 8

von Dobschütz 3

Cavallo 34, 35

**Plates***

**04 C**  C. Tischendorf, *Codex Ephraemi Syri rescriptus sive Fragmenta Novi Testamenti* (Leipzig, 1843) and plates (with full prolegomena and notes)

*The Beginnings of Christianity* vol. III, pt I, iv f. (for Acts)

A list of corrections of Tischendorf's edition, based on a fresh examination of the manuscript, was published by W. Lyon, 'A Re-examination of the Codex Ephraimi Rescriptus', *NTS* V (1958–9), 266–72

H. H. Oliver, 'A Textual Transposition in Codex C (Ephraemi Syri Rescriptus)', *JBL* LXXVI (1957), 233–6

Hansell I, II (full text in parallel with other uncials, and plates in III, nos. 1 and 2)

R. B. Stone, 'The Life and Hard Times of Ephraim Rescriptus', *Bible Today* (Collegeville, Minn.) 24 (1986), 112–18

**Plates**  Omont, *Facs* (1892), 3; (1896), 2

Sitterly (1898), 6

Hatch XX

A & A 6

Kenyon–Adams, *Our Bible*, XXV (i)

Vogels 7

Cavallo 82

Plates*

05 D  The text was first published by T. Kipling, *Codex Theodori Bezae Cantabrigiensis* (2 vols., Cambridge, 1793). Critical edn with introduction and notes by F. H. A. Scrivener, *Bezae Codex Cantabrigiensis being an exact copy in ordinary type ... edited with a critical introduction, annotations and facsimiles* (Cambridge, 1864; reprinted, Pittsburgh Reprint Series 5, 1978)

Hansell I, II (full text in parallel with other uncials)

For a photographic reproduction of the codex see *Codex Bezae Cantabrigiensis Quattuor Evangelia et Actus Apostolorum complectens Graece et Latine Sumptibus Academiae phototypice repraesentatus* (Cambridge, 1899).[3] A convenient presentation of the distinctive text of Codex Bezae (collated against the Gebhardt–Tischendorf edition of the New Testament) was given by Eberhard Nestle in his *Novi Testamenti supplementum* (Leipzig, 1896), pp. 7–66. English translations of codex Bezae have been published by William Whiston, *The Primitive New Testament* (London, 1745);

Johannes Greber, *The New Testament: a New Translation and Explanation Based on the Oldest Manuscripts* (New York, 1937);

J. M. Wilson, *The Acts of the Apostles, Translated from the Codex Bezae with an Introduction on its Lucan Origin and Importance* (London, 1923)

Among older studies the following are a selection:

[R. Porson,] 'Codex Theodori Bezae Cantabrigiensis', *British Critic* (London, February 1794), 139–47, 361–73

D. Schulz, *Disputatio de codice D Cantabrigiensi* (Bratislava, 1827)

---

[3] See review by F. G. Kenyon, *JTS* I (1899), 293–9.

J. Rendel Harris, *Codex Bezae: a study of the so-called Western Text of the New Testament, Texts and Studies*, vol. II, pt 1 (Cambridge, 1891)

J. Rendel Harris, *Four Lectures on the Western Text of the New Testament* (London, 1894)

E. Nestle, 'Some Observations on the Codex Bezae', *Ex*, Fifth Series I (1895), 235–40

F. H. Chase, *The Old Syriac Element in the Text of Codex Bezae* (London, 1893); and *The Syro-Latin Text of the Gospels* (London, 1895)

J. Rendel Harris, *The Annotators of the Codex Bezae* (London, 1901)

John Chapman, 'The Order of the Gospels in the Parent of Codex Bezae', *ZNW* VI (1905), 339–46

John Chapman, 'The Original Contents of Codex Bezae', *Ex*, Sixth Series XII (1905), pp. 46–53

H. J. Vogels, *Die Harmonistik im Evangelientext des Codex Cantabrigiensis. Ein Beitrag zur neutestamentlichen Textkritik*, *T & U* 36/1a (Berlin, 1910)

E. A. Lowe, 'The Codex Bezae', *JTS* XIV (1913), 385–8[4]

Many articles on all aspects of the MS are to be found in *The Bulletin of the Bezan Club* (12 vols., Leiden, 1926–37)

The following are a selection of some more recent studies of the Codex:

A. C. Clark, *The Primitive Text of the Gospels and Acts* (Oxford, 1914)

A. C. Clark, *The Acts of the Apostles* (Oxford, 1933), pp. 173–220 (review by K. and S. Lake, *JBL* LII (1934), 34–45). (See also text set out for Acts

---

[4] E. A. Lowe's other *Kleinschriften* are collected in *Palaeographical Papers (1907–1965)* ed. L. Bieler (2 vols., Oxford, 1972).

in vol. III of *Beginnings of Christianity* and
pp. lvi–lxxxiv)[5]

F. G. Kenyon, 'The Western Text in the Gospels
and Acts', *Proceedings of British Academy* XXIV
(London, December 1938), 287–315

M.-J. Lagrange, *Critique textuelle* II, *La Critique
rationelle* (Paris, 1935), pp. 42–67, 389–401

W. H. P. Hatch, *The 'Western' Text of the Gospels*
(Evanston, 1937)

O. Stegmüller, 'Zu den Bibelorakeln im Codex
Bezae', *Biblica* 34 (1953), 13–22

A. F. J. Klijn, *A Survey of the Researches into the
Western Text of the Gospels and Acts* (Leiden,
1949) and in *Nov T* 3 (1959), 1–27, 169–73; and
id., *A Study of the Researches into the Western
Text of the Gospels and Acts*, pt II, *Supplements* to
*Novum Testamentum* XXI, (Leiden, 1969)

J. D. Yoder, *The Language of the Greek Variants
of Codex Bezae Cantabrigiensis* (Ann Arbor, 1958)

P. Glaue, 'Einige Stellen die die Bedeutung des
Codex D charaktiesiert', *Nov T* 2 (1958), 310–15

J. D. Yoder, 'The Language of the Greek Variants
of Codex Bezae', *Nov T* 3 (1959), 241–8

J. D. Yoder, 'Semitisms in Codex Bezae', *JBL* 78
(1959), 317–21

J. D. Yoder, *Concordance to the Distinctive Greek
Text of Codex Bezae*, NTTS 2 (Leiden and Grand
Rapids, 1961)

E. J. Epp, 'The "Ignorance Motif" in Acts and
Antijudaic Tendencies in Codex Bezae', *HTR* 55
(1962), 51–62

E. J. Epp, *The Theological Tendency of Codex
Bezae Cantabrigiensis in Acts*, SNTS 3 (Cambridge,
1966)

---

[5] The book of Acts according to Codex Bezae was translated by A.
Bornemann, *Acta Apostolorum ab Sancto Luca conscripta ad Codicis
Cantabrigiensis* ... (Grossenhain, 1848).

E. J. Epp, 'Coptic Manuscript G67 and the Rôle of Codex Bezae as a Western Witness in Acts', *JBL* LXXXV (1966), 199–212

B. M. Metzger, 'The Influence of Codex Bezae upon the Geneva Bible of 1561', *NTS* 8 (1961–2), 72–7 (and in B. M. Metzger, *Historical and Literary Studies*, *NTTS* 8 (Leiden, 1968), pp. 138–44 and 1 plate)

M. Mees, 'Die Änderungen und Zusätze im Matthäusevangelium des Codex Bezae', *Vet Chr* 4 (1967), 107–29

M. Mees, 'Lukas 1–9 in der Textgestalt des Codex Bezae', *Vet Chr* 5 (1968), 89–110

M. Mees, 'Jesusworte im Lukas 12 und ihre Komposition nach Codex Bezae Cantabrigiensis', *Vet Chr* 7 (1970), 285–303

D. C. Parker, 'A Dictation Theory of Codex Bezae', *JSNT* 15 (1982), 97–112

H. W. Bartsch, 'Über den Umgang der früher Christenheim mit der Text der Evangelien. Das Beispiel des Codex Bezae Cantabrigiensis', *NTS* 29 (1983), 167–82

J. S. MacKenzie, 'The Latin Column in Codex Bezae', *JSNT* 6 (1980), 58–76

H.-W. Bartsch, *Codex Bezae versus Codex Sinaiticus in Lukasevangelium* (Hildersheim, 1983)

E. Bammel, 'The Cambridge Pericope. The Addition to Luke 6.4 in Codex Bezae', *NTS* 32 (1986), 404–26

E. Delebecque, *Les deux Actes des Apôtres, Etudes Bibliques* 6 (Paris, 1986)

J. N. Birdsall, 'The Geographical and Cultural Origin of the Codex Bezae Cantabrigiensis: A Survey of the Status Quaestionis, mainly from the Palaeographical Standpoint', in *Studien zum Text und zur Ethik des Neuen Testament*, ed. W. Schrage, *BZNW* 47 (Berlin and New York, 1986), pp. 102–14

G.J.C. Jordaan, 'Variation in Word Order between
the Greek and Latin Texts in Codex Bezae', in
*A South African Perspective on the New Testament*,
ed. J.H. Petzer and P.J. Hartin (Leiden, 1986),
pp. 99–111

Plates  Hatch XXII

von Dobschütz 4 and 5

Kenyon–Adams, *Our Bible*, XXVI

Sitterly (1898), 7

Kenyon (1912), VI

Metzger, *Text*, 5

Finegan 18

Metzger, *Manuscripts*, 19

Pal Soc I, 14, 15

A & A 9 and 10

Vogels 18

Cavallo 60

Plates*

*Additional note*

Some general articles on the background of Codex
Bezae are:

K. Lake, 'On the Italian Origin of Codex Bezae, I,
Codex Bezae and Codex 1071', *JTS* I (1900),
441–5; F.E. Brightman, 'On the Italian Origin of
Codex Bezae II. The Marginal Use of Lections',
*JTS* I (1900), 446–54; F.C. Burkitt, 'The Date of
Codex Bezae', *JTS* III (1902), 501–13; H. Quentin,
'Le Codex Bezae à Lyon au IX$^e$ siècle? Les
Citations du Nouveau Testament dans le
martyrologie d'Adon', *R Bén* 23 (1906), 1–25; G.
Mercati, 'On the Non-Greek Origin of the Codex
Bezae', *JTS* XV (1914), 448–51; E.A. Lowe, 'The
Codex Bezae and Lyons', *JTS* XXV (1924), 270–4
and 2 plates; F.C. Burkitt, 'Codex Bezae and the
"Sortes Sangallenses"', *JTS* XXVIII (1927), 58 f.;
R.C. Stone, 'The Language of the Latin Text of
Codex Bezae', *Illinois Studies in Language and*

|        |        |
|--------|--------|
|        | *Literature* XXX, 2–3 (Urbana, 1946); J. Mizzi, 'The Vulgate Text of the Supplemental Pages of Codex Bezae Cantabrigiensis', in *Sacris erudiri* XIV (Steenbrugge, 1963), 149–63 (see also id., 'The African Element in the Latin Text of Matt. XXIV of Codex Cantabrigiensis', *R Bén* 78 (1968), 33–66) |
| 06 D   | C. Tischendorf, *Codex Claromontanus* (Leipzig, 1852) |
|        | Hansell II (full text in parallel with other uncials) and plates in III, nos. 3 and 4 |
|        | A. Souter, 'The Original Home of Codex Claromontanus, (D Paul)', *JTS* VI (1904–5), 240–3 |
|        | J. M. Bover, 'Textus Codicis Claromontani in epistola and Galatas', *Biblica* XII (1931), 199–218 |
|        | H. J. Vogels, 'Der Codex Claromontanus der Paulinischen Briefe', in H. G. Wood (ed.), *Amicitiae corolla* (Harris Festschrift) (London, 1933), pp. 274–99 |
|        | Treu, pp. 38–9 |
| Plates | Pal Soc, I 63/64 |
|        | von Dobschütz 4 and 5 |
|        | Vogels 20 |
|        | Hatch XXX |
|        | Cavallo 61 |
|        | Omont, *Facs* (1892), 5 (of Latin side); (1896), 7 |
| Plates* | |
| 06 abs | Description and plate in B. Montfaucon, *Palaeographia Graeca* (Paris, 1708), pp. 218–20. Facsimiles of this manuscript are given by J. S. Semler in his edition of J. J. Wettstein's *Prolegomena* (1764, nos. 8, 9) (see also G. Bianchini, *Evangeliarium quadruplex* II, pp. 591–2) |
|        | J. J. Griesbach, *Symbolae criticae* II (Halle, 1793), pp. 75–7 |
| 07 E   | Russell Champlin, *Family E and its Allies in Matthew*, *S & D* XXIII (Salt Lake City, 1967) |

J. Geerlings, *Family E and its Allies in Mark*, *S & D* XXXI (Salt Lake City, 1968)

J. Geerlings, *Family E and its Allies in Luke*, *S & D* XXXV (Salt Lake City, 1968) and plates

F. Wisse, 'Family E and the Profile Method', *Biblica* 51 (1970), 67–75

Plates     Hatch XXXVIII

Metzger, *Text*, 8

Cavallo 97

(Fam. E may include F (010), G (012), H (013), U (020) and Ω (045). Geerlings includes variants from S (028), V (031), 44, 65, 98, 219 and 422.)

08 E     Thomas Hearne, *Acta apostolorum Graeco-Latine ... e codice Laudiano ...* (Oxford, 1715) and plate IX

Edited by C. Tischendorf, *Codex Laudianus*, *Mon sac* IX, and plate

Hansell II (full text in parallel with other uncials) and plate in III, no. 5

O. K. Walther, 'Codex Laudianus G 35: A Re-Examination of the Manuscript, Including a Reproduction of the Text and an Accompanying Commentary', Unpublished Ph.D. dissertation, University of St Andrews, 1979

J. H. Ropes, 'The Greek Text of Codex Laudianus', *HTR* XVI (1923), 175–86 (see also *Beginnings of Christianity* III, pp. lxxxiv–lxxxviii)

A. C. Clark, *The Acts of the Apostles* (Oxford, 1933), pp. 234–46

E. A. Lowe, 'An Eighth-Century List of Books in a Bodleian ms. from Würzburg and its Probable Relation to the Laudian Acts', *Sp* 3 (1928), 3–15

B. R. Motzo, 'Beda e il codice laudiano degli Atti', *RR* 3 (1927), 453–6

M.-J. Lagrange, *Critique textuelle* II, *La Critique rationelle* (Paris, 1935), pp. 401–2

R.L. Poole, 'A Stage in the History of the Laudian ms. of Acts', *JTS* XXIX (1928), 399–400

(In his essay *Expositio Retracta* Bede gives seventy and more readings, all of which are in this manuscript, and often only in this. See M.L.W. Laistner, 'The Latin Versions of Acts Known to the Venerable Bede', *HTR* XXX (1937), 37–50.)

|          |                                                                            |
|----------|----------------------------------------------------------------------------|
| Plates   | Metzger, *Text*, 6a                                                         |
|          | Metzger, *Manuscripts*, 22                                                  |
|          | Scrivener, *Intr*, 3rd edn, X, nr.25; *Intr*, 4th edn, vol.1, facing p.121  |
|          | Wilson 4                                                                    |
|          | Pal Soc I, 80                                                               |
|          | Vogels 22                                                                   |
|          | Hatch XXXIII                                                                |
|          | Cavallo 93                                                                  |

Plates*

09 F      Description and collation in J. Heringa, *Disputatio de Codice Boreeliano nunc Rheno-Trajectino*, ed. H.E. Vinke (Utrecht, 1843)

Plates      Hatch LVII

010 F      Tischendorf, *Anecdota*, pp.209–16

         Scrivener, *Exact Transcript* and plate

Plates      Pal Soc I, 127

         Vogels 23

         Hatch L

(010      See 07 (fam E))

010 (+ 012)   F(+G)   On their relationship: W.B. Smith, *AJT* 7 (1903), 452–85, 662–88

010 (+ 012)   F(+G)   W.H.P. Hatch, 'On the Relationship of Codex Augiensis and Codex Boernerianus of the Pauline Epistles', *Harvard Studies in Classical Philology* LX (1951), 187–99 (see also J.B. Lightfoot, *Journal of Philology* 2 (London and Cambridge, 1869), 292, and 3 (1871) 210; id., *St. Paul's Epistles to the Colossians and to Philemon*,

8th edn (London, 1886), p.345; F.J.A. Hort,
*Journal of Philology* 3 (1871), 67ff.; Paul Corssen,
*Epistularum paulinarum codices Graece et Latine
scriptos, Specimen* 1 (Kiel, 1887), 2 (1889);
Friedrich Zimmer, *Zeitschrift für Wissenschaftliche
Theologie* 30 (1887), 76–91, and id., *TLZ* 15
(1890), cols. 59–62)

011 G     Extracts in J.C. Wolf, *Anecdota graeca* (Hamburg,
1723), III, pp.48–92

Plates     J. Geerlings, *Family E and its Allies in Luke*, S & D
XXXV (Salt Lake City, 1968), plate III

Hatch LVIII

012 G     C.F. Matthaei, *XIII epistolarum Pauli codex
Graecus cum versione latine veteri vulgo
Antehieronymiana olim Boernerianus nunc
bibliothecae electoralis Dresdensis* (Meissen, 1791)
and 2 plates. Plate also in id., *Ev. sec. Matt. Gr. et
Lat.* (Riga, 1788)

Photographic reproduction with introduction by A.
Reichardt, *Der Codex Boernerianus* (Leipzig, 1909)

Franz Delitzsch, *Zeitschrift für die gesammte
lutherische Theologie und Kirche* (Leipzig, 1866),
pp.281–92; (1882), pp.488–509; (1883), pp.73–99,
309–44

Plates     Vogels 25

Metzger, *Manuscripts*, 28

A & A 33

(012     See 07 (fam E))

(012     On the relationship of 010 and 012 see 010)

(013     See 07 (fam E))

013 H

Plates     Hatch LIX

014 H     Tischendorf, *Mon sac* I, pp.37–44 and plates I, II,
V and VI (see also H.A. Sanders, 'New Manuscripts
of the Bible from Egypt', *Amer J Arch* XII (1908),
49–55 and two plates; E. Nestle 'Zum Freer
Logion', *Th Lit* XXX (1909), pp.353–5)

| | |
|---|---|
| Plates | Vogels 8 |
| | Hatch LII |
| 015 H | Matthaei (as 'frag vetus') |

Montfaucon, pp. 253 ff.

Tischendorf, *Mon sac*, VIII

L. Duchesne, 'Fragments des Epîtres de S. Paul', in *Archives des Missions scientifiques et littéraires*, Series 3, vol. 3 (Paris, 1876), pp. 420–9

B. Peyron, 'Di due frammenti greci delle epistole di san Paolo del V o VI secolo che si conservano nella biblioteca nationale di Torino', *Atti della R. Accademia delle scienze di Torino* 15 (Turin, 1879), vol. 4, pp. 493–8

A. Ehrhard, 'Der Codex H ad epistolas Pauli et "Euthalius Diaconus"', *Centralblatt für Bibliothekswesen* 8 (1891), 388 ff.

J. A. Robinson, *Euthaliana, Texts and Studies* 3, no. 3 (Cambridge, 1895), pp. 48–71

Henri Omont, 'Notice sur un très ancien manuscrit grec en onciales des épîtres de saint Paul, conservé à la bibliothèque nationale (H ad epistulas Pauli) par H.O.' (cf. *Notices et extraits des manuscrits de la bibliothèque nationale* 33 (Paris, 1890), pp. 141–92) (Paris, 1889) and 2 plates

K. Lake, *Facsimiles of the Athos Fragments of the Codex H of the Pauline Epistles* (Oxford, 1905)

M.-J. Lagrange, *Critique textuelle* II, *La Critique rationelle* (Paris, 1935), pp. 467–8

H. S. Murphy, 'On the Text of Codices H and 93', *JBL* 78 (1959), 228–37 and 1 plate (and cursive 88)

Treu, pp. 31–4

| | |
|---|---|
| Plates | B. Montfaucon, *Nouveau traité de diplomatique* (Paris, 1750), I, p. 687; plate XII, no. 1 |

Silvestre II, pp. 63–4

Savva, pp. 1–4 and plate A

Omont, *Facs* (1892), 4; (1896), 6

Hatch XXXII

Plates
016 I   Caspar René Gregory, *Das Freer Logion*, *Versuche und Entwürfe* 1 (Leipzig, 1905) and plate on p. 23

H. A. Sanders, *The New Testament Manuscripts in the Freer Collection*, pt II, 'The Washington Manuscript of the Epistles of Paul', University of Michigan Studies, Humanistic Series, vol. IX, transcription, 3 facsimiles (New York and London, 1918)

M.-J. Lagrange, *Critique textuelle* II, *La Critique rationelle* (Paris, 1935), pp. 468–9

Clark, *USA*, pp. 205–6

Plates   Hatch XXXI

Cavallo 83

Plates*

(016   see also 032)

017 K   Collation by J. M. A. Scholz, *Curae criticae in historiam textus evangeliorum* (Heidelberg, 1820), pp. 80–90

W. Bousset, 'Die Groupe K Π (M) in den Evangelien', in *Textkritische Studien zum Neuen Testament*, *T & U* 11, 4 (Leipzig, 1894), pp. 111–85

Description: B. Montfaucon, *Palaeographia Graeca* (Paris, 1708), pp. 41, 231–3 and plate

Bianchini, *Evang quadr* (Rome, 1749), pt 1, vol. 2, p. DIII and plate

W. H. P. Hatch, 'A Redating of Two Important Uncial Manuscripts of the Gospels – Codex Zacynthius and Codex Cyprius', in Lake F/S, pp. 337 f.

Plates   Hatch LXXV

Plate II in R. Champlin, *Family Π in Matthew*, *S & D* XXIV (Salt Lake City, 1964)

Omont, *Facs* (1892) 17/2; (1896) 5

Plates*

(017   See 041 fam. Π)

| | |
|---|---|
| 018 K | Matthaei (as g) |
| | J. Leroy, 'Un témoin ancien des petits catéchèses de Théodore Studite', *Scriptorium* 15 (1961), 36–60 |
| | Treu, pp. 280–3 |
| Plates | Hatch LXIII |
| | Metzger, *Text*, 9 |
| 019 L | Tischendorf, *Mon sac* (1846), proleg., pp. 15–24; *Text*, pp. 57–399 and 2 plates |
| Plates | Omont, *Facs* (1892), 16/2; (1896), 4 |
| | Kenyon (1912), VII |
| | A & A 34 |
| | Hatch XXXIX |
| Plates* | |
| 020 L | Description: B. Montfaucon, *Palaeographia Graeca* (Paris, 1708) |
| | Bianchini, *Evang quadr* |
| | G. Mucchio, *Studi italiani di filologia classica* 4, *Index Codicum Bibliothecae Angelicae* no. 39 (Florence, 1896), pp. 7–184, esp. p. 81 |
| Plates | Hatch XLVIII |
| 021 M | Description: B. Montfaucon, *Palaeographia Graeca* (Paris, 1708), p. 260 and fac. |
| | Description by R. Champlin in appendix B of R. Champlin, *Family E and its Allies in Matthew*, S & D XXVIII (Salt Lake City, 1967), pp. 163–9 |
| Plates | Silvestre II, no. 76 |
| | Omont, *Facs* (1892), 17/1; (1896), 5 |
| | Hatch XLVI |
| | Cavallo 113 |
| Plates* | |
| 022 N | Rome portions, ed. Bianchini, *Evang quadr* pt 1, vol. 2, pp. DIa–DIIIa |
| | Scrivener, *Full and Exact Collation*, p. xl (as j) |
| | London, Vienna and Vatican Fragments in |

Tischendorf, *Mon sac* (Leipzig, 1846), proleg., pp. 10 ff.; *Text*, pp. 11 ff.; plates II, nos. 2, 3 and 4

H. S. Cronin, *Codex Purpureus Petropolitanus. The text of Codex N of the gospels edited with an introduction and an appendix*, Texts and Studies, vol. 5, no. 4 (Cambridge, 1899)

Patmos portions, ed. L. Duchesne, *Archives des missions scientifiques et littéraires* (Paris, 1876), vol. 3, pp. 386–419 (with plates)

Athens and New York portions ed. by S. Rypins, 'Two Inedited Leaves of Codex N', *JBL* 75 (1956), 27–39 and 2 plates

J. Cozza-Luzi, *Nova patrum bibliotheca* vol. X pt 3 (Rome, 1905), pp. 21–6

A. Vaccari, 'Codicis Evangeliorum purpurei N due folia nuper detecta', *Biblica* 37 (1956), 528–30 (see also A. Vaccari, 'Codicis Evangeliorum Purpurei N folium iterum repertum', *Biblica* 12 (1931), 483 f.)

F. B. Adams, 'A Sixth-Century Pierpont Morgan Leaf', 7th Annual Report to the Fellows of the Pierpont Morgan Library (New York, 1957), pp. 11–14

Treu, pp. 169–73

Plates    Hatch XXIX

Kenyon, *Facsimiles*, IV

New Pal Soc I, 151

W. Hartel and F. Wickhoff, *Die Wiener Genesis* (Vienna/Prague/Leipzig, 1895), 49–52

Vogels 9

Seider II, p. 167 and plate XXXVI

Pattie 8

Cavallo 86, 87, 88

Plates*

023 O    H. Omont, 'Notice sur un très ancien manuscrit grec de l'évangile de saint Matthieu ...', *Notices et extraits des manuscrits de la bibliothèque*

*nationale* ..., vol. 36 (Paris, 1901), pp. 599–676 and 2 plates; id., 'Un nouveau feuillet du codex Sinopensis', *Journal des savants* (Paris, 1901); id., *Monuments et mémoires publiés par l'Académie des Inscriptions et Belles-Lettres*, Fondation Eugène Piot, vol. 7, pt 2, pp. 175–86; plates 16–19

Adolf Harnack, *TLZ* 14 (1900), cols. 411–13

E. von Dobschütz, *Literarisches Centralblatt* 24 (Leipzig, 1900), col. 1028

H. S. Cronin, 'Codex Chrysopurpureus Sinopensis', *JTS* II (1901), 590–600

| | |
|---|---|
| Plates | Hatch XXVIII |
| | Cavallo 89 |

On the miniatures see: H. Omont, *Monuments et memoires publiés par l'Académie des Inscriptions et Belles-Lettres*, Fondation Eugène Piot, vol. 7, 175ff. and plates XVI–XIX; id., *Fac-similes des miniatures des plus anciens manuscrits grecs de la Bibliothèque Nationale du VI$^e$ au XI$^e$ siècle* (Paris, 1902), pp. 1 ff.

Plates*

| | |
|---|---|
| 024 P | Tischendorf, *Mon sac* VI, pp. xii–xiv, xvi, xvii, 249–338; and plate in vol. III (1860), no. 2 |
| Plates | A & A 19 |
| | Cavallo 92 |
| Plates* | |
| 025 P | Tischendorf, *Mon sac* V, pp. 1 ff. and VI, pp. 1 ff. |
| | Hoskier, *Text*, 1.7 |
| | Treu, pp. 101–4 |
| Plates | Hatch LI |
| | Cereteli and Sobolewski II, 41 |
| 026 Q | Tischendorf, *Mon sac* III, pp. xxxvi–xxxix, 262–90 and plate II |
| Plates | Cavallo 66 |
| Plates* | |
| 027 R | Tischendorf, *Mon sac* II, pp. xiv–xxii, 1–92, and plate no. 1 |

(corrections by S.P. Tregelles, in Horne's
*Introduction*, 11th edn (London, 1863), pp. 764ff.)

New leaves: W. Wright, *Journal of Sacred
Literature* III (London, 1864), 466

Two extra leaves published by Gregory, *Textkritik*
III, *Nachtrag*, pp. 1024–5

Plates      Kenyon, *Facsimiles* 3 (see also *Catalogue of ancient
mss in the Br. Mus.* 1, pl. X)

Kenyon (1912), VIII

Pattie 4

Hatch XXVI

Cavallo 79

Plates*

028 S      Description: Bianchini, *Evang quadr* with plate
preceding p. cdxciii (see also pp. dlxxi–dlxxii)

Plates      New Pal Soc I, 105

Cavalieri and Lietzmann 13

Hatch LXIX

Metzger, *Manuscripts*, 31

Lefort and Cochez 78

Plates*

(028      See 07 (fam E)

029 T      The text of the fragment of John was edited by
A.A. Georgi, *Fragmentum evangelii S. Johannis
Graecum Copto-Sahidicum* ... (Rome 1789) with
plate.

G. Balestri (ed.), *Sacrorum bibliorum fragmenta
copto-sahidica Musei Borgiana*, *Novum
Testamentum* III (Rome, 1904), pp. 202–18,
234–60

A. Hebbelynck, 'Les Manuscrits coptes-sahidiques
du Monastère Blanc', *Muséon* 2 (1912), 70

P. Franchi de'Cavalieri, *Codices graeci Chisiani et
Borgiani* (Rome, 1927), pp. 141–3

Clark, *USA*, pp. 161–2

| | |
|---|---|
| Plates | Cavalieri and Lietzmann 3 |
| | Vogels 46 |
| | Hatch XXIII |
| 030 U | |
| Plates | Hatch LXII |
| Plates* | |
| (030 | See 07 (fam E)) |
| 031 V | Matthaei (as V) |
| | Treu, pp. 235–8 |
| Plates | C. F. Matthaei, *Novum Testamentum Graece et Latine* (Riga, 1782–8), IX, pp. 265 ff.; and XII, 2 plates at end of volume |
| | Sabas, p. 4 and plate B |
| | Hatch XLV |
| Plates* | |
| 032 W | C. R. Gregory, *Das Freer-Logion, Versuche und Entwürfe* I (Leipzig, 1905), pp. 13–23, 25–66 and 3 plates |
| | Adolf Harnack, 'Neues zum unechten Marcusschluss', *TLZ* XXXIII, no. 6 (1908), cols. 168–70 |
| | C. Schmid, *TLZ* XXXIII, no. 12 (1908), cols. 359–60 |
| | H. A. Sanders, *The New Testament Manuscripts in the Freer Collection*, pt I, 'The Washington Manuscript of the Four Gospels', University of Michigan Studies, Humanistic Series, vol. IX. Collation and 4 plates (London and New York, 1916; with pt II, London and New York, 1918) |
| | H. A. Sanders (ed.), *Facsimile of the Washington Manuscript of the Four Gospels in the Freer Collection* (Ann Arbor, 1912) |
| | Edgar J. Goodspeed, *AJT* XVII (1913), 240–9, 395–411 (collation of Matthew), 599–613 (collation of John); XVIII (1914), 131–46 (collation of Luke, Mark 1–4); 266–81 (collation of Mark 5–16) |

H.C. Hoskier, 'The New Codex W', *Ex* VII (1913), 467–80, 515–31

E. Jacquier, 'Le Manuscript Washington des Evangiles', *Rev bib* 10 (1913), 547–55

Edgar J. Goodspeed, *The Freer Gospels* (Chicago, 1914) (collation against Westcott and Hort)

Alexander Souter, 'The Freer (Washington) Ms. of the Gospels', *Ex* VIII (1914), 350–67

Edgar J. Goodspeed, *Greek Gospel Texts in America* (*HLS* Ser. 1), vol. II, *Texts*, pp. 53–117 (reprint of the *Freer Gospels* (1914))

Subsequent studies on the manuscript, its textual character and its readings include:

A.J. Edmunds, 'The Washington Manuscript and the Resurrection in Mark', *Mo* 28 (1918), 528–9

P.E. Kretzmann, 'The Freer Manuscripts and the Oxyrhynchus Papyri', *TM* 1 (1921), 255–9

A.T. Robertson, 'Some Interesting Readings in the Washington Codex', *Ex* III (1925), 192–8

B.H. Streeter, 'The Washington Manuscript of the Gospels', *HTR* XIX (1926), 165–72 (see also C.A. Phillips, 'The Washington Ms. of the Gospels by Dr. Streeter', *BBC* 5 (1928), 9–12 (a summary and critique of Streeter's article)

K. Lake, R.P. Blake and S. New, 'The Caesarean Text of the Gospel of Mark', *HTR* XXI (1928), 207–404

F.C. Burkitt, 'Studies in the Western Text of St. Mark', *JTS* XVII (1916), 139 (see 038: Burkitt)

B.H. Streeter, 'The Washington Ms. and the Caesarean Text of the Gospels', *JTS* XXVII (1926), 144–7 (largely a rebuttal of Burkitt's objections to Streeter's views regarding the unity of the Caesarean text)

M.J. Lagrange, *Critique textuelle* II, *La Critique rationelle* (Paris, 1935), pp. 144–9

B. Botte, 'Freer (Manuscrits de la collection)', in *Dictionnaire de la Bible, Supplément* 3 (ed. L. Pirot) (Paris, 1938), cols. 527–30

C.S.C. Williams, 'Syriacisms in the Western Text of Mark', *JBL* 42 (1941), 177 f.

Clark, *USA*, pp. 201–5

B.H. Streeter, 'W and the Caesarean Text', in id., *The Four Gospels*, 2nd edn (London, 1926), pp. 598–600

Eugen Helzle, 'Der Schluss der Markusevangeliums und das Freerlogion (Mk. 16, 14 W)', dissertation, Tübingen, 1959 (see also *TLZ* (1960), cols. 470 f.)

L.W. Hurtado, *Codex Washingtonianus in the Gospel of Mark; its Textual Relationships and Scribal Characteristics*, Ph.D. dissertation, Case Western Reserve University, 1973

L.W. Hurtado, *Text-Critical Methodology and the Pre-Caesarean Text Codex W in the Gospel of Mark*, *S & D* XLIII (Grand Rapids 1981)

Plates　　Milligan VI

Cavello 108

von Dobschütz 8

On the miniatures: C.R. Morey, 'East Christian Paintings in the Freer Collection', *Studies in East Christian and Roman Art*, *University of Michigan Studies, Humanistic Series* 12, pt 1 (New York, 1914), pp. 63–81

New Pal Soc I, 201

Kenyon–Adams, *Our Bible*, XXVII

Hatch XXI

Vogels 5

Clark 39

Finegan 19 and 20

Metzger, *Manuscripts*, 16

A & A 35

Plates*

(032　　　See also 016)

| | |
|---|---|
| 033 X | |
| Plates | Scrivener, *Intr*, 4th edn, opposite p. 343 |
| | Vogels 10 |
| | Hatch LXXI |
| Plates* | |
| 034 Y | Gregory, *Textkritik* III, pp. 1027–37 |

W. C. Braithwaite, 'A New Uncial of the Gospels', *ET* XIII (1901), pp. 114 ff.; id., 'The Lection System of the Codex Macedonianus', *JTS* V (1904), 265–74

R. Champlin, 'Codex Y and Family Π' = appendix A of R. Champlin, *Family E & its Allies in Matthew*, *S & D* XXVIII (Salt Lake City, 1967), pp. 156–62

Plates    Hatch XLIX

035 Z    John Barrett, *Evangelium secundum Matthaeum ex codice rescripto in bibliotheca collegii ssae Trinitatis iuxta Dublinum* (Dublin, 1801)

S. P. Tregelles, *The Dublin codex rescriptus: a supplement* (London, 1863)

T. K. Abbott, *Par palimpsestorum Dublinensium. The codex rescriptus Dublinensis of St. Matthew's gospel (Z) ... a new edition revised and augmented* (London, 1880)

Hansell I and III, appendix II, p. 313 (full text in parallel with other uncials)

T. K. Abbott, 'On An Uncial Palimpsest Evangelistarium', *Hermathena* X (1884), 146–50; id., 'On a Fragment of an Uncial Lectionary', ibid., pp. 151–3; id., 'On a Greek Biblical Fragment', *Hermathena* XVII (1891), 233–5

John Gwynn, 'On the External Evidence Alleged against the Genuineness of St. John XXI. 25', *Hermathena* XIX (1893), 368–84

A. H. McNeile, 'Some Early Canons', *JTS* XXVIII (1927), 225–32

J.G. Smyly, 'Notes on Greek Mss. in the Library of Trinity College', *Hermathena* XLVIII (1933), 163–95

| | |
|---|---|
| Plates | Hatch XXIV |
| Plates* | |
| 036 Γ | Tischendorf, *Anecdota*, pp. 5f. and plate I, 4 and id., *Notitia*, p. 53 |
| | Treu, pp. 41–3 |
| Plates | Pal Soc II, 7 |
| | Hatch LXI |
| Plates* | |
| 037 Δ | H.C.M. Rettig, *Antiquissimus quatuor evangeliorum canonicorum Codex Sangallensis Graeco-Latinus interlinearis* (Zurich, 1836) |
| | J. Rendel Harris, *The codex Sangallensis (Δ). A Study in the Text of the Old Latin Gospels* (London, 1891) |
| | O. von Gebhardt, 'Eine angeblich verborgene griechisch-lateinische Evangelienhandschrift', *ZBW* 10 (1893), 28–35 |
| Plates | Pal Soc I, 179 |
| | von Dobschütz 9 |
| | Hatch LXV |
| | Metzger, *Text*, 13a |
| | Vogels 24 |
| Plates* | |
| 038 Θ | Facsimile edition of the text of Mark, *Materialy po Arkheologii Kavkaza* ... xi (Moscow, 1907) |
| | Transcription of the entire text in Gustav Beermann and Caspar Rene Gregory, *Die Koridethi Evangelien Θ 038* (Leipzig, 1913) |
| | A. Souter, 'The Koridethi Gospels', *Ex* VIII/10 (1915), 173–81 |
| | F.C. Burkitt, 'W and Θ: Studies in the Western Text of St. Mark', *JTS* XVII (1916/17), 1–21, 139–52 |

J. De Zwaan, 'No Coptic in the Koridethi Codex', *HTR* 18 (1925), 112–14. See also R.P. Blake, *HTR* 18 (1925), 114 and 25 (1932), 273–6

B. Botte, 'Koridethi (Évangiles de)', in *Dictionnaire de la Bible, Supplément*, ed. L. Pirot and A. Robert, Fasc. 24 (Paris, 1950) cols. 192–6

K. Lake and R.P. Blake, 'The Text of the Gospels and the Koridethi Codex', *HTR* XVI, 3 (1923), 267–86 (see also *HTR* 21 (1928), 207 ff.)

H.C. Hoskier, 'Collation of Koridethi with Scrivener's Reprint of Stephen III', *BBC* 6 (1929), 31–56 (covers only Mark 1–5)

B.H. Streeter, *The Four Gospels* (London, 1924), pp. 77–107, 572–84

P.E. Kretzmann, 'The Koridethi Manuscript and the Latest Discoveries in Egypt', *Concordia Theological Monthly* 3 (St Louis, Mo., 1932), pp. 574–8

Treu, pp. 351–3
(see also J.N. Birdsall, *Classical Review* XXXIII (Oxford, 1987), 305–6)

Plates    A & A 36

Hatch XLIV

Metzger, *Manuscripts*, 25

Plates*

039 Λ     Tischendorf, *Notitia*, pp. 58 f.

Tischendorf, *Anecdota*, p. 45 I, no. III and plate

Alfred Rahlfs, 'Über eine von Tischendorf aus dem Orient Mitgebrachte, in Oxford, Cambridge, London and Petersburg liegende Handschrift der Septuaginta', *Nachrichten der K. Gesellschaft der Wissenschaften zu Göttingen. Phil-hist. Klasse* I (1898), pp. 98–112

E. von Dobschütz, 'Zwei Bibelhandschriften mit doppelter Schriftart', *TLZ* 24 (1899), col. 74 (on the link with 566)

P. Gächter, 'Codex D and Λ', *JTS* XXXV (1934), 248–66

| | |
|---|---|
| | Treu, pp. 48–50 |
| Plates | Wilson 7 |
| | Vogels 14 |
| | von Dobschütz 10 |
| | Hatch LIV |
| Plates* | |
| 040 Ξ | S. P. Tregelles, *Codex Zacynthius* (London, 1861) |
| | N. Pocock, 'The Codex Zacynthius', *The Academy* (London, 19 February 1881), pp. 136c–137c |
| | J. H. Greenlee, 'The Catena of Codex Zacynthius', *Biblica* 40 (1959), 992–1001 |
| | J. H. Greenlee, 'A Corrected Collation of Codex Zacynthius (Cod. Ξ)', *JBL* LXXVI (1957), 237–41; id., 'Some Examples of Scholarly "Agreement in Error"', *JBL* LXXVII (1958), 363–4 |
| | W. H. P. Hatch, 'A Redating of Two Important Uncial Manuscripts of the Gospels – Codex Zacynthius and Codex Cyprius', in Lake F/S, pp. 333–8 |
| Plates | Hatch XXV |
| 041 Π | Tischendorf, *Notitia*, pp. 51 f. |
| | S. Lake, *Family Π and the Codex Alexandrinus: The Text According to Mark*, *S & D* V (London 1937) |
| | J. Geerlings, *Family Π in Luke*, *S & D* XXII (Salt Lake City, 1962); id., *Family Π* in John, *S & D* XXIII (Salt Lake City, 1963) |
| | R. Champlin, *Family Π in Matthew*, *S & D* XXIV (Salt Lake City, 1964) and 1 plate |
| | W. Bousset, 'Die Gruppe K, Π (M) in den Evangelien', in *Textkritische Studien zum Neuen Testament*, *T & U* 114 (Leipzig, 1894), pp. 111–35 |
| | Treu, pp. 43–5 |
| Plates | Hatch LII |
| (041 | Fam Π can include: |
| | K (017), 265, 489, 1009, 1079, 1200, 1219, 1223, 1313 and others) |

042 Σ     O. von Gebhardt and A. Harnack, *Evangeliorum Codex Graecus Purpureus Rossanensis* (Leipzig, 1880)

O. von Gebhardt, *Die Evangelien des Matthäus und des Marcus aus dem Codex Purpureus Rossanensis*, *T & U* I 4 (Leipzig, 1883)

W. Sanday, *The Text of Codex Rossanensis (Σ)*, *Studia biblica* I (Oxford, 1885), pp. 103–12

P. F. Russo, *Il Codice Purpureo di Rossano* (Rome, 1954)

Plates     A study of the manuscript in its artistic aspects, with photographic reproductions of all the miniatures, was published by A. Haseloff, *Codex Purpureus Rossanensis* (Berlin and Leipzig, 1898). Another full reproduction, with the plates in colour, was edited by A. Muñoz, *Il codice purpureo di Rossano* (Rome, 1907)

Metzger, *Text*, 7

A & A 37

Hatch XXVII

Plates*

043 Φ     G. T. Stokes, in *Ex*, Series III, vol. 3 (London, 1886), pp. 78ff.

P. Batiffol (description), 'Evangeliorum codex Graecus purpureus Beratinus Φ', in *Mélanges d'archéologie et d'histoire, de l'école française de Rome* 5 (Paris and Rome, 1885), pp. 358–76; and id. (full description with plates), 'Les Manuscrits grecs de Bérat d'Albanie et le codex purpureus Φ', *Archives des missions scientifiques et littéraires*, 3rd Series, vol. 13 (Paris, 1887), pp. 467–556

J. Koder, 'Zur Wiederentdeckung zweier Codices Beratini', *Byz Z* 65 (1972), 327–8

Plates*

044 Ψ     K. Lake, *Texts from Mount Athos*, *Studia biblica et ecclesiastica* 5 (Oxford, 1902), pp. 89–185 (text of Mark and collation of Luke and John). Cf. id., 'The Text of Ψ in St. Mark', *JTS* I (1900), 290–2

|          | Gregory, *Textkritik* I, pp. 94−5 |
|----------|-----------------------------------|
|          | M.-J. Lagrange, *Critique textuelle* II, *La Critique rationelle* (Paris, 1935), pp. 109−10 |
| Plates   | Hatch XLII |
|          | Cavallo 90 |
|          | Metzger, *Manuscripts*, 24 |
| 045 Ω    | M.-J. Lagrange, *Critique textuelle*, II, *La Critique rationelle* (Paris, 1935), pp. 141−2 |
|          | Collated by M. W. Winslow in *Six Collations* and 1 plate |
| Plates   | Hatch LXIV |
| (045     | See 07 (fam. E)) |
| 046      | Described with reproductions by S. P. Tregelles, *An Account of the Printed Text* (London, 1854), pp. 156 ff. |
|          | Tischendorf, *Mon sac* (1846), pp. 407 ff. and plate III, no. 9; id., *Appendix Novi Testamenti Vaticani* (Leipzig, 1869), pp. iii ff. and 1 ff. |
|          | A. Mai, *Novum Testamentum Graece ex antiquissimo Codice Vaticano* (Rome, 1859), pp. 465 ff. |
|          | Giuseppe Cozza, *Ad editionem Apocalypseos s. Johannis ... Lipsiae anno 1869 evulgatam animadversiones* (Rome, 1869) |
|          | Hansell II (full text in parallel with other uncials) |
| Plates   | Hatch LXX |
| 047      | Collation by W. Sanday, 'Étude critique sur le Codex Patiriensis du Nouveau Testament', *Rev bib* IV (1895), 207−13; see also J. H. Greenlee, 'A Corrected Collation of Codex Zacynthius (Cod Ξ)', *JBL* LXXVI (1957), 237−41 (cf. 040) |
|          | Clark, *USA*, pp. 61−3 |
| Plates   | Vikan 2 |
|          | Clark 7 |
|          | A & A 38 |
|          | Hatch LX |

Metzger, *Manuscripts*, 23

| | |
|---|---|
| Plates* | |
| 048 | Bianchini, *Evang quadr* |
| | P. Batiffol, *L'Abbaye de Rossano* (Paris, 1891), pp. 62, 71 ff. (Variorum reprint, Geneva, 1971) |
| | D. Heath, 'The Text of Manuscript Gregory 048 (Vatican Greek 2061)', Privately circulated Ph.D. thesis, Taylor University, 1965 |
| 049 | |
| Plates | Hatch XLIII |
| 050 | Matthaei (as 15) |
| | Ed. Tregelles as an appendix to his edition of Ξ (see 040) |
| | B. Ehlers, 'Eine Katene zum Johannes-Evangelium in Moskau, auf dem Athos (Dionysiu), in Athen and in Oxford (050)', *ANTF* 3, pp. 96–133 |
| | Treu, pp. 262–4 |
| Plates | Wilson 29 |
| Plates* | |
| 051 | Gregory, *Textkritik* III, pp. 1042–6 |
| | Hoskier, *Text*, 1, pp. 2–4 |
| 052 | Gregory, *Textkritik* III, pp. 1046 f. |
| | Hoskier, *Text* 1, p. 5 |
| 054 | Tischendorf, *Mon sac* (1846), *proleg.*, p. 13; Text, pp. 37 ff. and plate III, no. 5 |
| Plates | Hatch XLI |
| 055 | J. Burgon, *The Last Twelve Verses of Mark* (London, 1871), pp. 282–7 |
| 056 | Tischendorf, *Mon sac* (1846) and plate III, no. 8 |
| 057 | A. H. Salonius, 'Die griechischen Handschriftenfragmente des Neuen Testaments in den Staatlichen Museen zu Berlin', *ZNW* 26 (1927), 97–119 (see also 060, 0109, 0160, 0165, 0188, and 0189) |
| Plates | A & A 16 |

| | |
|---|---|
| 058 | Gregory, *Textkritik* I, pp. 72–3 |
| 059 | Gregory, *Textkritik* I, pp. 73–4 |
| Plates | Cavallo 46b |
| 060 | A. H. Salonius, *Handschriften*, pp. 102–4 (see 057) |
| 061 | T. Zahn, *Forschungen zur Geschichte des neutestamentlichen Kanons* III, *Supplementum Clementinum* (Erlangen, 1884), pp. 277–8. |
| | B. Reicke, 'Les Deux Fragments grecs onciaux de I Tim. appelés 061 publiés', *Coniectanea Neotestamentica* 11 (Uppsala, 1947), 196–206 and plates |
| 062 | W. H. P. Hatch, 'An Uncial Fragment of the Gospels', *HTR* 23 (1930), 149–52 |
| 063 | Treu, pp. 294–5 |
| | Gregory, *Textkritik* III, pp. 1048–60 |
| | K. Treu, 'Remarks on some Uncial Fragments of the Greek NT', in *Studia evangelica* III, *T & U* 88 (Berlin, 1964), p. 280 |
| 064 | Treu, pp. 111–12 |
| | Gregory, *Textkritik* III, pp. 1363–8 |
| 065 | (and 066, 067, 078, 079, 096, 097) |
| | Published as $I^{1-7}$ by Tischendorf in *Mon sac* I, pp. xiii–xix and 1–48 and plate I (see also Tischendorf, *Anecdota*) |
| | Treu, pp. 18–19 |
| 066 | Treu, pp. 19–20 |
| | Text in Tischendorf, *Mon sac* I, pp. xiii–xix and pp. 43 ff. |
| 067 | Tischendorf, *Mon sac* I, pp. xiii–xix, 1–48 and plate I, no. III |
| | Treu, pp. 22–4 |
| 068 | Tischendorf, *Mon sac* II, pp. xxxii f., 311–12 and 2 plates |
| 069 | Grenfell and Hunt, *OP* I, 7 |
| | Gregory, *Textkritik* I, p. 68 |

Clark, *USA*, pp. 272–3

070 H. Ford, *Appendix ad editionem Novi Testamenti Graeci e Codice MS Alexandrino a C. G. Woide descripti* (Oxford, 1799), pp. 52–62, 83.

(The following bilinguals are now considered to be part of 070: 0110, 0124, 0178, 0179, 0180, 0190, 0191, 0193, 0194 and 0202)

071 Grenfell and Hunt, *OP* 3, pp. 1–2

Clark, *USA*, pp. 116–17

073 J. R. Harris, *Biblical Fragments from Mt Sinai* (London, 1890), pp. x, 16 (= [6] – [12] and [14]) (Also 074, 092, 0112, 0118, 0119, 0137 and 0140)

Treu, pp. 113–14

C. R. Gregory, *Textkritik* III, p. 1027

Plates Hatch XLIX

074 J. R. Harris, *Biblical Fragments from Mt Sinai* (London, 1890), pp. xi, xii, 27–44

Treu, pp. 111–12

076 B. P. Grenfell und A. S. Hunt, *The Amherst Papyri, being an account of the Greek Papyri in the collection of Lord Amherst of Hackney at Didlington Hall, Norfolk* I (London 1900), pp. 41–3

Clark, *USA*, p. 171

077 J. R. Harris, appendix to Agnes Smith Lewis, *Studia Sinaitica* no. 1 (London, 1894), p. 98, no. 5

078 Treu, pp. 21–2

Ed. Tischendorf, *Mon sac* I, pp. xii–xix, 5–10, 17 f., 23 f., 27 f. and 35 f. and plate I, no. 4

Plates*

079 Tischendorf, *Mon sac* I, pp. xiii–xix, 21 f. and 25 f. and Tischendorf, *Anecdota*, plate III, no. VI

Treu, pp. 30–1

080 Treu, pp. 110–11

081 Treu, pp. 24–5

Brief description in Tischendorf, *Notitia*, p. 50 ('primum')

Plates*

082       Treu, pp. 292–3

Plates*

083       Brief description in Tischendorf, *Notitia*, p. 50 ('secundum')

(083,      and others including 0112 and 0235: see J. Irigoin, 'L'Onciale greque de type copte', *Jahr öster byz Gesell* 8 (1959), 29–51)

Plates*

084       Treu, pp. 113–14

085       Treu, pp. 192–3

Some readings in Gregory, *Textkritik* III, pp. 1061f.

(085:      On 085, 099, 0100, 0113, 0114, 0124, 0125, 0127, 0128, 0129 and 0139 see Amélineau, *Notice*, pp. 362–428)

086       W. E. Crum and F. G. Kenyon, 'Two Chapters of St John in Greek and Middle Egyptian', *JTS* I (1899–1900), 415–33

087       Brief description in Tischendorf, *Notitia*, p. 50 ('quartum')

Treu, pp. 28–30

I. A. Sparks (on the fragment bound into *l* 852), 'A New Uncial Fragment of St Matthew', *JBL* 88 (1969), 201–2

Plates*

088       Tischendorf, *Mon sac* I, pp. xiii–xix, 45–8 and plate I, no. III

Treu, pp. 20–1

089       Treu, p. 115

090       Treu, pp. 111–12

091       Gregory, *Textkritik* III, p. 1063

Treu, p. 114

092       J. R. Harris, *Biblica Fragments from Mount Sinai* (London, 1890), pp. xii, 45–7

Treu, pp. 28–30, 115

093    C. Taylor, *Hebrew Greek Cairo Genizah Palimpsest from the Taylor-Schechter Collection including a fragment of the twenty-second Psalm according to Origen's Hexapla* (Cambridge, 1900), pp. 94–6 and plate XI

094    Gregory, *Textkritik* III, pp. 1063–5

095    Brief description in Tischendorf, *Notitia*, p. 50 ('quintum')

Plates    Hatch XXXVII

096    Tischendorf, *Mon sac* I, pp. 37 f., 41 f. and plate I, no. 5

Treu, pp. 37–8

Plates*

097    Tischendorf, *Mon sac* I, pp. 39 f. and plate I, no. 6

Treu, pp. 36–7

Plates*

098    J. Cozza, *Sacrorum Bibliorum vetustissima fragmenta Graeca et Latina ex palimpsestis codicibus bibliothecae Cryptoferratensis eruta* (Rome, 1867), pp. 332–5

099    Gregory, *Textkritik*, I, pp. 70–1

Amélineau, *Notice*, pp. 402–4; see also pp. 370–1; plate

G. Horner, *Sahidic* 1, pp. 640–2; see also K. Treu, *Bilinguen*, p. 114

0100    Amélineau, *Notice*, pp. 372 f., 407

0101    Gregory, *Textkritik* I, pp. 74–5

0102    H. Omont, *Catalogue des manuscrits grecs, latins, français, et espagnols, et des portulans recueillis par feu Immanuel Miller* (Paris, 1897), pp. 1, 2, 95–8 and plate I (see also 0117)

0103    J. H. Greenlee, *Nine Uncial Palimpsests of the New Testament*, S & D XXXIX (Salt Lake City, 1968) and plate

0104    J. H. Greenlee, *Nine Uncial Palimpsests of the New Testament*, S & D XXXIX (Salt Lake City, 1968)

| 0105 | Text in Gregory, *Textkritik* III, pp. 1066–74 |
| Plates | Hatch XXXIV |
| Plates* | |
| 0106 | Tischendorf, *Mon sac* (1846) *proleg.*, pp. 9 f.; text, pp. 1 ff. and plate I, no. 1; and *Mon sac* II, pp. xxxxvi f., 321 |
| Plates | Hatch XXXVI |
| Plates* | |
| 0107 | Brief description in Tischendorf, *Notitia*, p. 50 ('tertium') |
| | Treu, pp. 27–8 |
| Plates | Hatch XXXV |
| Plates* | |
| 0108 | Brief description in Tischendorf, *Notitia*, p. 50 ('sextum') |
| | Treu, pp. 39–40 |
| 0109 | A. H. Salonius, *Handschriften*, p. 108 (see also 057) |
| | U. Wilcken, *Tafeln zur älteren Griechischen Paläeographie* (Leipzig/Berlin, 1891), p. x and plate VI |
| 0110 | Published by Amélineau, *Notice*, pp. 366–9, 380–99 (see also 0200, 0198) |
| | H. J. M. Milne (ed.), *Catalogue of the Literary Papyri in the British Museum* (London, 1927), pp. 180–4 (re-edits 0200, 0110, and 0198) |
| 0111 | Gregory, *Textkritik* III, p. 1075; see also A. H. Salonius, 'Die griechischen Handschriften des neuen Testaments in den Staatlichen Museen zu Berlin', *ZNW* 26 (1927), 97–119 (see also 057) |
| 0112 | Brief description in Tischendorf, *Notitia*, p. 50 ('secundum') |
| | J. R. Harris, Appendix in Agnes Smith Lewis, *Studia Sinaitica* no. 1 (London, 1894), pp. 103, 104 and plate 7 |
| | J. R. Harris, *Biblical Fragments from Mount Sinai* (London, 1890), pp. xii, xiii, 48–52 |

|        | Treu, pp. 25–7 |
|--------|----------------|
| 0113   | Amélineau, *Notice*, pp. 369–72, 401–2, 404–5 |
| 0114   | Amélineau, *Notice*, p. 373; text = pp. 407–8 |
| 0115   | Tischendorf, *Mon sac* (1846), *proleg.*, pp. 13 f.; text, pp. 51 ff.; plate III, no. 6 |
| Plates | Omont, *Facs* (1892), $16^1$; (1896), 4 |
|        | Hatch XL |
| Plates* | |
| 0116   | C. Tischendorf, *Jahrbuch der Literatur* 117 (Vienna, 1847), 8 f. (repeated by Angelo Antonio Scotti, *Memorie della reg. accad. Ercolanense di archeologia* (Naples, 1852), vol. 4) |
| 0117   | H. Omont, *Catalogue des manuscripts grecs, latins, français et espagnols et des portulans recueillis par feu Immanuel Miller* (Paris, 1897), pp. 2, 99–102 |
|        | Treu, pp. 294–5 |
| 0118   | J. Rendel Harris, *Biblical Fragments from Mount Sinai* (London, 1890), pp. x, 15 |
| 0119   | J. R. Harris, *Biblical Fragments from Mount Sinai* (London, 1890), pp. xi, 17–24 |
|        | Treu, pp. 34–5 |
| 0120   | Five sheets published by Joseph Cozza, *Sacrorum bibliorum vetustissima fragmenta Graeca et Latina e codicibus Cryptoferratensibus eruta* III (Rome, 1877), pp. cxxi–cxxxiv |
|        | Fragment (6th sheet) published by Gregory, *Textkritik* III, pp. 1078–9 |
| 0121   | London fragments published by Tischendorf, *Anecdota* (Leipzig, 1855), pp. 174–89, 190–205. Corrected in second edition (Leipzig, 1861), pp. 177–205. |
|        | J. N. Birdsall, 'The Two Fragments of the Epistles designated M (0121)', *JTS* XI (1960), 336–8 (see also Birdsall: cursive 1739) |
| 0122   | Treu, pp. 40–1 |
| 0123   | Treu, pp. 35–6 |

| | |
|---|---|
| 0124 | Published by Amélineau, *Notice*, pp. 366−9, 380−99 and 6 plates |
| 0125 | Published by Amélineau, *Notice*, pp. 372, 406−7 |
| 0127 | Published by Amélineau, *Notice*, pp. 373−4, 408−9 |
| 0128 | Published by Amélineau, *Notice*, pp. 409−10; see also p. 374 and plate |
| 0129 | Published by Amélineau, *Notice*, pp. 410−11; see also pp. 374−5 (See also *l* 1575) |
| 0130 | Alban Dold, 'Neue Palimpsest-Bruchstücke der griechischen Bibel; Zwei bekannte neugelesene Palimpsest-Bruchstücke einer St Galler Evangelienhandschrift', *BZ* 18 (1929), 241−70 (see also 0197) |
| | Tischendorf, *Mon sac* III (1860), *proleg.*, p. iii, pp. xxxix, xl; text, pp. 291−8, plate II |
| 0131 | Scrivener, *Adversaria* (as W[d]) |
| | J. Rendel Harris, *The Diatessaron of Tatian* (London/Cambridge, 1890), pp. 62−8 and 2 plates |
| | J. Duplacy, 'La Provenance athonite des manuscrits grecs légués par R. Bentley à Trinity College, Cambridge et en particulier de l'oncial 0131 du Nouveau Testament', in B. L. Daniels and M. J. Suggs (eds.), *Studies in the History and Text of the New Testament in Honor of K. W. Clark*, *Studies and Documents 29* (Salt Lake City, 1967), pp. 457−68 reprinted in J. Delobel (ed.), *Études de critique textuelle du Nouveau Testament*, *Bibliotheca ephemeridum theologicarum Lovaniensium* LXXVIII (Louvain, 1987), pp. 55−68 |
| 0132 | A. A. van Sittart, *J of Phil* II (1869), 241 |
| | J. H. Greenlee, *Nine Uncial Palimpsests of the New Testament*, *S & D* XXXIX (Salt Lake City, 1968) and plate |
| 0133 | Announced by J. P. Mahaffy, 'An uncial MS of the Gospels', *Athenaeum* (London, 2 July 1881), 14bc |
| | Described by T. K. Abbott (with photographs and readings), *Hermathena* X (Dublin, 1884), 146−50 (see also 035) |

0133 (and *l* 334)

Plates*

0134      J. H. Greenlee, *Nine Uncial Palimpsests of the New Testament*, *S & D* XXXIX (Salt Lake City, 1968) and plate

0135      J. H. Greenlee, *Nine Uncial Palimpsests of the New Testament*, *S & D* XXXIX (Salt Lake City, 1968)

0136      Treu, pp. 116–17

0137      J. R. Harris, *Biblical Fragments from Mount Sinai* (London, 1890), pp. xi, 25, 26

        Treu, pp. 116–17

0139      Published by Amélineau, *Notice*, pp. 369–71, 399–402

0140      A. S. Lewis, *Studia Sinaitica* I (London, 1894), p. 116

0143      V. Reichmann, 'Ein Unzialfragment in Oxford', *ANTF* 3, pp. 193–8

0144      W. H. P. Hatch, 'An Uncial Fragment of the Gospels', *HTR* 23 (1930), 149–52

0149      Text in A. Deissmann, *Veröffentlichungen aus der Heidelberger Papyrus-Sammlung* I (Heidelberg, 1905), pp. 81 f. and collation, pp. 83 f.

0152      = $T^1$ ($T^2$) (T = Talisman)

        On $T^1$ see von Dobschütz, p. 86

        $T^3$ $T^4$ see *ZNW* 25 (1926), 300

        $T^5$ $T^6$ see *ZNW* 27 (1928), 218

        $T^7$ $T^8$ $T^9$ see *ZNW* 32 (1933), 188

        $T^{10}$ O'Callaghan's apparatus, Bover–O'Callaghan, *Nuevo Testamento Trilingüe* (Madrid, 1977)

        Clark, *USA*, pp. 139, 226–7 (= $T^2$)

        T. Zahn, *Kommentar* [*Matthäus*] (Leipzig, 1905), p. 269, n. 66 (= $T^3$) (see also Ulrich Wilcken, 'Heidnisches und Christliches aus 'Agypten', *APF* I (1901), 396–436)

        *PSI* 6, pp. 151–2 (= $T^4$)

Friedrich Bilabel, 'Griechische Papyri', in
*Veröffentlichungen aus den Badischen Papyrus-Sammlungen* 4 (Heidelberg, 1924), pp. 49–52
(= $T^5$)

E. Schäfer, *Papyri Jandanae* I (Leipzig, 1912),
pp. 18–32 (= $T^6$)

C. Wessely, *Stud zur Pal und Pap* 20 (Leipzig,
1921), p. 141 (= $T^8$)

0153      (= $O^{1-20}$) (O = Ostraka)

J. G. Tait, *Greek Ostraka in the Bodleian Library
and Various other Collections* (London, 1930), esp.
p. 145 (= on 1 Jn 29–14, 21–2)

G. Lefebvre, 'Fragments grecs des Évangiles sur
Ostraca', *Bulletin de l'institut français d'archéologie
orientale* 4 (Cairo, 1940), 1–15

Rudolf Knopf, 'Eine Tonscherbe mit den Text des
Vaterunsers', *Mitteilungen des kaiserlichen
deutschen archäologischen Institüts zu Athen* 25
(1900), 313–24; id., *ZNW* 2 (1901), 228–33

0160      A. H. Salonius, *Handschriften*, pp. 99–100 (see
057)

Description and plates by O. von Gebhardt and A.
Harnack, *Evangeliorum codex Graecus Purpureus
Rossanensis* (Leipzig, 1880)

Text edited by O. von Gebhardt, *Die Evangelien
des Matthäus und des Marcus aus dem Codex
Purpureus Rossanensis, T & U* I 4 (Leipzig, 1883)

Plates     A. Haseloff, *Codex Purpureus Rossanensis: Die
Miniaturen der griechischen Evangelien-Handschrift
in Rossano nach photographischen Aufnahmen
herausgegeben von A. H.* (Berlin/Leipzig, 1898)

0162      J. M. Bover, 'Dos papiros egipcios del N.T.
recientemente publicados', *EE* 9 (1930), 291–320

Clark, *USA*, p. 135

Grenfell and Hunt, *OP* VI, pp. 4–5 and plate VI

0163      Grenfell and Hunt, *OP* VI, p. 6 and plate I

Text repeated in R. H. Charles, *Revelation of St
John* II, *ICC* (Edinburgh, 1920), pp. 449–51

Clark, *USA*, p. 273

Hoskier, *Text*, p. 1

0164 Text published in Gregory, *Textkritik* III, p. 1083

J. Leipoldt, 'Bruchstücke von zwei griechisch-koptischen Handschriften des Neuen Testament', *ZNW* 4 (1903), 350–1

0165 Text in Gregory, *Textkritik* III, pp. 1368–71

A. H. Salonius, *Handschriften*, pp. 110–15 and plate (see also 057)

0166 Text in A. Deissmann, *Die Septuagintapapyri und andere altchristliche Texte der Heidelberger Papyrussammlung* (Heidelberg, 1905), p. 85

0167 K. Treu, 'Neutestamentliche Unzialfragmente in einer Athos-Handschrift 0167 Lavra, Δ 61', *ZNW* 54 (1963), 53–8

M. McCormick, 'Un fragment inédit de lectionnaire du VIII$^e$ siècle', *R Bén* 86 (1976), 76–82

K. Treu, 'Nochmals zu dem Unzialfragment 0167', *ZNW* 55 (1964), 133

M. McCormick, 'Two Leaves from a Lost Uncial Codex 0167 Mark 4$^{24-29}$; 4$^{37-41}$', *ZNW* 70 (1979), 238–42

M. McCormick, 'Palaeographical Notes on the Leaves of St Mark from Louvain', *Scriptorium* 34 (1980), 240–7 and 4 plates

0169 Grenfell and Hunt, *OP* VIII, pp. 14f.

Text repeated in R. H. Charles, *Revelation of St John* II, *ICC* (Edinburgh, 1920), II, pp. 448–50

Clark, *USA*, p. 177

Plates Metzger, *Text* 6b

Milligan VIII

Metzger, *Manuscripts*, 12

0170 Grenfell and Hunt, *OP* IX, pp. 5–7 and XI, p. 251 app.

Clark, *USA*, pp. 177–8

0171 *PSI* I, pp. 2–4 and II, pp. 22–5

M.-J. Lagrange, *Critique textuelle* II, *La Critique rationelle* (Paris, 1935), pp. 71–6 (inc. collation)

J.M. Bover, 'Un fragmento de San Lucas (22, 4–63) en un papiro recientemente descubierto', *EE* 4 (1925), 293–305

Wessely, *Patr or* XVIII (1924), p. 452–4

Described by Naldini, *Documenti*, nos. 11–12 and plate

Treu, *APF* 18 (1966), 25–8

K. Aland, 'Alter und Entstehung des D-Textes in Neuen Testament. Betrachtung en zu P69 und 0171', in *Miscel-lània papirològica Ramon Roca-Puig*, ed. S. Janeras (Barcelona, 1987), pp. 37–61

| | |
|---|---|
| Plates | A & A 18 |
| | Horsley, pp. 125–40 |
| 0172 | *PSI* I, 4 (see also Naldini, *Documenti*, no. 19 and plate) |
| 0173 | *PSI* I, 5 (see also Naldini, *Documenti*, no. 21 and plate) |
| 0174 | *PSI* II, 118 (see also I. Crisci, *Papiri di Firenze* 91) |
| 0175 | *PSI* II, 125 (see also Cavallo, p. 115) |
| | (see also Naldini, *Documenti*, no. 16 and plate) |
| 0176 | *PSI* II, 251 (see also Naldini, *Documenti*, no. 18 and plate) |
| 0177 | W. Till, 'Papyrussammlung der Nationalbibliothek in Wien: Katalog der Koptischen Bibelstücke. Die Pergamente', *ZNW* 39 (1940), 1–56 (also 0178, 0179, 0180, 0190, 0191, 0237, 0238) |

The text of the following MSS is found in C. Wessely, *Stud zur Pal und Pap*:

0177 XI 55b
0178 XI 56b
0179 XI 57b
0180 XI 58c
0181 XII 185
0182 XII 188

|      |                |
|------|----------------|
| 0183 | XII 192 and fac. |
| 0184 | XV 232 |
| 0185 | XV 235 and fac. |
| 0186 | XV 256 and fac. |
| 0189 | XII 139 |
| 0190 | XII 140 |
| 0191 | XII 186 |
| 0192 | XII 187 |
| 0193 | XII 189 |

0180    J. Irigoin, *Jahr österr byz Gesell* 8 (1959), 29–51 and plate, p. 41

Plates    Cavallo 104

(0181, 0182, 0183, 0184, 0185, 0186: See 0177 (Wessely))

(0186    See 0124, Klos)

0187    A. Deissmann (ed.), *Veröffentlichungen aus der Heidelberger Papyrussammlung* I (Heidelberg, 1905), and 1 plate

0188    A. H. Salonius, 'Die griechischen Handschriftenfragmente des Neuen Testaments in den Staatlichen Museen zu Berlin', *ZNW* 26 (1927), 100–2

K. Treu, 'Zur vermeintlichen Kontraktion von ΙΕΡΟΣΟΛΥΜΑ in 0188, Berlin p. 13416', *ZNW* 52 (1961), 278–9

0189    Published by A. H. Salonius, 'Die griechischen Handschriftenfragmente des Neuen Testaments in den Staatlichen Museen zu Berlin', *ZNW* 26 (1927), 116–19 and plate

Plates    A & A 32

(0189, 0190, 0191, 0192, 0193: See 0177 (Wessely))

0193    Published by Horner, *Sahidic* 3, p. 348

0194    Published by Amélineau, *Notice*, pp. 380–99; see also pp. 366–9

0196    W. H. P. Hatch, 'An Uncial Fragment of the Gospels', *HTR* 23 (1930), 149–52

(0197    See 0130, Dold)

| | |
|---|---|
| (0198 | See 0110, Milne) |
| (0200 | See 0110, Milne) |
| 0201 | W. E. Crum and H. I. Bell, *Coptica* III: *Wadi Sarga; Coptic and Greek Texts, from the Excavations Undertaken by the Byzantine Research Account* (Copenhagen, 1922), pp. 32–42 |
| 0203 | (see *l* 1575) |
| 0204 | A. Passoni dell'Acqua, *Aegyptus* 60 (1980), 110–19 and plate 6 (collation) |
| 0206 | Grenfell and Hunt, *OP* XI (1915), pp. 5–6 |
| | Clark, *USA*, p. 13 |
| 0207 | M.-J. Lagrange, *Critique textuelle* II, *La Critique rationelle* (Paris, 1935), pp. 585–6 |
| | J. Schmid, 'Der Apokalypsetext des Kodex 0207 (Papiri della Società Italiana 1166)', *BZ* 23 (1935/36), 187–9 |
| | G. Vitelli and G. Mercati, *PSI* 10, pp. 112–20 (see also Naldini, *Documenti*, no. 22 and plate) |
| 0208 | A. Dold, 'Griechische Bruchstücke der Paulusbriefe aus dem 6. Jahrhundert unter einem Fragment von Prospers Chronicon aus dem 8. Jahrhundert', *Zentralblatt für Bibliothekswesen* 50 (1933), 76–84 |
| 0209 | K. W. Clark, *USA*, p. 277 |
| | J. H. Greenlee, *Nine Uncial Palimpsests of the New Testament*, *S & D* XXXIX (Salt Lake City, 1968) and plate |
| 0210 | O. Stegmüller, 'Zu den Bibelorakeln im codex Bezae', *Biblica* 34 (1953), 13–22 |
| 0211 | Treu, pp. 349–51 |
| Plates | Hatch LV |
| Plates* | |
| 0212 | Carl H. Kraeling, *A Greek Fragment of Tatian's Diatessaron from Dura*, *S & D* III (London, 1935) (facsimile, transcription, and introduction) |
| | F. C. Burkitt, 'The Dura Fragment of Tatian', *JTS* XXXVI (1935), 255–9 |
| | Hans Lietzmann, 'Neue Evangelienpapyri', *ZNW*, XXXIV (1935) 291–3 (with transcription) |

M.-J. Lagrange, 'Deux nouveaux textes relatifs à l'évangile', *Rev bib* XLVI (1935), 321–7 (with transcription and facsimile)

D. Plooij, 'A Fragment of Tatian's Diatessaron in Greek', *ET* XLVI (1935), 471–6 (with transcription)

M. I. Rostovtzeff, *The Excavations at Dura-Europos Conducted by Yale University and the French Academy of Inscriptions and Letters* (New Haven, 1935), pp. 416 f.

A. Baumstark, 'Das Griechische Diatessaron-Fragment von Dura Europos', *Oriens Christ* 10 (1978), 244–52

C. B. Welles, R. O. Fink, and J. F. Gilliam, 'The Parchments and Papyri', *Excavation Report* V, pt i (New Haven, 1959), pp. 23–4

Appendix I to M.-J. Lagrange, *Critique textuelle II, La Critique rationelle* (Paris, 1935), pp. 627–33

G. D. Kilpatrick, *'Dura-Europos: The Parchments and the Papyri', Greek, Roman and Byzantine Studies* 5 (Cambridge, Mass., 1964), pp. 215–25

Clark, *USA*, p. 375

| | |
|---|---|
| Plates | A & A 14 |
| | Metzger, *Manuscripts*, 8 |
| 0213 | P. Sanz, 'Griechische literarische Papyri christlicher Inhalte', *Mitteilungen aus der Papyrussammlung der Nationalbibliothek in Wien* 4 (Vienna, 1946) (Also 0219, 0221–8) |
| Plates | Cavallo 91 b |
| 0215 | |
| Plates | Cavallo 46 a |
| 0216 | |
| Plates | Cavallo 57 a |
| 0219 | Horsley, pp. 125–40 |
| 0220 | W. H. P. Hatch, 'A Recently Discovered Fragment of the Epistle to the Romans', *HTR* 45 (1952), 81–5 |

| | |
|---|---|
| Plates 0221 | A & A 15 |
| Plates 0222 | Cavallo 49a |
| Plates | Cavallo 58b |
| (0224 0226 | On the link with 0186 see Aland, *TLZ* 78 (1953), col. 469 (report by H. Klos) |
| Plates 0227 | Cavallo 49b |
| Plates 0229 | Cavallo 58a |
| | G. Mercati, *PSI* XIII, pp. 1, 8–11 and plate 1 (see also I. Crisci, 'La Collezione dei Papiri di Firenze', in *Proceedings of the XII Congress of Papyrology* (Toronto, 1970), pp. 89–95, esp. p. 93 and Naldini, *Documenti*, no. 23 and plate) |
| 0230 | Published by G. Mercati, *PSI* XIII, pp. 87–102 and plate 6 (see also Naldini, *Documenti*, no. 20 and plate) |
| | N. A. Dahl, '0230 ( = PS1 1306) and the Fourth-century Greek–Latin Edition of the Letters of Paul', in *Text and Interpretation* (ed. E. Best and R. McL. Wilson) (Cambridge, 1979), pp. 79–98 |
| 0231 | C. H. Roberts, *The Antinoopolis Papyri* I (London, 1950), pp. 23–4 and addenda |
| 0232 | C. H. Roberts, *The Antinoopolis Papyri* I (London 1950), pp. 24–6 and plate 1 |
| 0234 | H. von Soden, *Sitzb Berl Akad* 39 (1903), 825–30 |
| 0235 | C. Loparev, *Opisanie rukopisej imperator skago obščestva ljubitelej drevnej pis'mennosti* 3 (St Petersburg, 1899), pp. 171–2 |
| | V. Benešević, *Catalogus codd. mss. Graecorum qui in monasterio S. Catharinae in monte Sina asservantur* I (St Petersburg, 1911), p. 639 and plate 18 |
| 0236 | Treu, p. 333 |

P. Weigandt, 'Zwei griechisch-sahidische Acta-Handschriften: p.41 und 0236', *ANTF* 3, pp.72–95 (see also A. Hebbelynck, *Muséon* 35 (1922), p.9)

0237    C. Wessely, 'Ein fayumisch-griechisches Evangelien-fragment', *Wien Stud* 26 (1912), 270–4 and plate; id., *ZNW* 39 (1940), 49 and plate

0238    W. Till, 'Kleine Koptische Bibelfragmente', *Biblica* 20 (1939), 372

0239    H.L. Heller, 'Ein griechisch-koptisches Lukasfragment', *ANTF* 3, pp.199–203

0240    B.M. Metzger, 'A Hitherto Neglected Early Fragment of the Epistle to Titus', *Nov T* 1 (1956), 149f.

G. Zereteli, 'Un palimpseste grec du $V^e$ siècle sur parchemin (Epist. ad Fit. [sic] 1. 4–6, 7–9)', *Académie royale de Belgique: Bulletin de la classe des lettres* $V^e$ sér. 18 (1932), 427–32

Treu, pp.353–4

0241    J. Vernon Bartlet, 'A New Fifth-Sixth Century Fragment of 1 Timothy', *JTS* XVIII (1917), 309–11

0242    R. Roca-Puig, 'Un pergamino griego del Evangelio de San Mateo', *Emérita* 27 (1959), 59–73

0245    G. Garitte, *Muséon* 73 (Louvain, 1960), 239–58 (describes 0245 with a transcription of Georgian and Greek)

J.H. Greenlee, *Nine Uncial Palimpsests of the New Testament*, *S & D* XXXIX (Salt Lake City, 1968) and 2 plates

J.N. Birdsall, 'Two Notes of New Testament Palaeography, 2. The Preservation of New Testament ms. 0245 (Selly Oak Colleges, Mingana Georg. 7)', *JTS* XXVI (1975), 394–8

0247    J.H. Greenlee, *Nine Uncial Palimpsests of the New Testament*, *S & D* XXXIX (Salt Lake City, 1968)

0250    *Editio princeps* of 4 leaves by A.S. Lewis, *Codex Climaci rescriptus*, *Horae semiticae* 8 (Cambridge, 1909), pp.xxvii–xxxi

I. A. Moir, *Codex Climaci rescriptus Graecus (Ms. Gregory 1561, L)*, *Texts and Studies* NS, 2 (Cambridge, 1956) and 1 plate

Review by K. Junack, *TLZ* 82 (1957), cols. 355–8

0251     C. Römer, '3 Johannesbrief 12–15 Judasbrief 3–5' in R. Pintaudi (ed.), *Miscellanea papyrologica*, *Papyrologica Florentina* VII (Florence 1980) and plate 25

0252     R. Roca-Puig, 'Un pergamí grec de la lletra als Hebreus (Pap. Barcinonensis, *inv. n.* 6, Hebr. 6, 2–4, 6–7)', *Boletin de la Real Academia de Buenas Letras de Barcelona* 30 (1963–64), 241–5; and reprinted in *Helmantica* 16 (1965), 145–9 and plate

0253     Published from a photograph: K. Treu, 'Ein neues neutestamentliches Unzialfragment aus Damaskus (= 0253)', *ZNW* 55 (1964), 274–7

Horsley, pp. 125–40

0254     Published from a photograph: K. Treu, 'Ein Weiteres Unzialpalimpsest des Galaterbriefes aus Damaskus', *Studia evangelica* 5, *T & U* 103 (Berlin, 1968), 219–21

Horsley, pp. 125–40

0255     Two pages published from a photograph: K. Junack, 'Ein Weiteres neutestamentliches Unzialfragment aus Damaskus (0255)', *ANTF* 3, pp. 209–17

0256     K. Niederwimmer, 'Bisher unedierte Fragmente biblischen Inhalts aus der Sammlung Erzherzog Rainer', *Jahr österr byz Gesell* 14 (1965), 10–11

0259     K. Treu, 'Neue Neutestamentliche Fragmente der Berliner Papyrussammlung', *APF* 18 (1966), 23–38

Horsley, pp. 125–40

0260     K. Treu, 'Neue Neutestamentliche Fragmente der Berliner Papyrussammlung', *APF* 18 (1966), 38

K. Treu, 'Griechisch-koptische Bilinguen des Neuen Testaments', *Wissenschaftliche Zeitschrift der Martin-Luther-Universität* (Halle/Wittenberg, 1965), 95–123

Horsley, pp. 125–40

0261 K. Treu, 'Neue Neutestamentliche Fragmente der Berliner Papyrussammlung', *APF* 18 (1966), 23–38; 19 (1969), 185

Horsley, pp. 125–40

0262 K. Treu, 'Neue Neutestamentliche Fragmente der Berliner Papyrussammlung', *APF* 18 (1966), 23–38 (with plates); 19 (1969), 185

Horsley, pp. 125–40

0263 K. Treu, 'Neue Neutestamentliche Fragmente der Berliner Papyrussammlung', *APF* 18 (1966), 23–38 and plate

Horsley, pp. 125–40

0264 K. Treu, 'Neue Neutestamentliche Fragmente der Berliner Papyrussammlung', *APF* 18 (1966), 23–38; 19 (1969), 183

Horsley, pp. 125–40

0265 K. Treu, 'Neue Neutestamentliche Fragmente der Berliner Papyrussammlung', *APF* 18 (1966), 23–38; 19 (1969), 181

Horsley, pp. 125–40

0266 K. Treu, 'Neue Neutestamentliche Fragmente der Berliner Papyrussammlung', *APF* 18 (1966), 23–38 (with plate); 19 (1969), p. 182

Horsley, pp. 125–40

0267 R. Roca-Puig, 'Un pergamí grec de l'Evangeli de Sant Lluc', in *Miscel-lània Carles Cardó* (Barcelona, 1963), pp. 395–9

R. Roca-Puig, 'Dos fragmentos biblicos de la colección Papyri Barcinonenses', *Helmantica* 16 (1965), 139–44 and 2 plates (the other MS = 0252)

0268 K. Treu, 'Drei Berliner Papyri mit nomina sacra', *Studia patristica* 10, *T & U* 30 (1970), 30 and plate; reprinted in id., *APF* 21 (1972), 82

0269 Collation in J. H. Greenlee, 'Codex 0169: A Palimpsest Fragment of Mark', in J. K. Elliott (ed.), *Studies in New Testament Language and*

Text, *Nov T Supplements* XLIV (Leiden, 1976), pp. 235–8

0270 Collation and 2 plates in J. Smit Sibinga, 'A Fragment of Paul at Amsterdam (0270)', in T. Baarda, A. F. J. Klijn and W. C. van Unnik (eds.), *Miscellanea neotestamentica* I (Leiden, 1978), pp. 23–44

0274 J. M. Plumley and C. H. Roberts, 'An Uncial Text of St. Mark in Greek from Nubia', *JTS* XXVII (1976), 34–45, with 2 plates

W. H. C. Frend and I. A. Muirhead, 'The Greek Manuscripts from the Cathedral of Q'asr Ibrim', *Muséon* 89 (1976), 43–9

G. M. Browne, 'The Sunnarti Mark', *ZPE* 66 (1986), 49–52

0275 Collated by A. Passoni dell'Acqua, *Aegyptus* 60 (1980), 102–6 and plate

0277 P. Prunetti, *Trenta testi Greci da papiri letterari e documentari*, (Florence, 1983), pp. 7–9 (Proceedings of the XVII Congresso Internationale di Papirologia (Naples, 1983))

# CURSIVES

| | |
|---|---|
| 1<sup>eap</sup> | K. Lake, *Codex 1 of the Gospels and its Allies*, *Texts and Studies* VII 3 (Cambridge, 1902) |
| Plates | Hatch LX |
| | Scrivener, *Intr*, 3rd edn, IX, p. 23 and 4th edn, I, p. 137 |
| | A & A 40 |
| Plates* | |
| (Family 1 | See also 22, 118, 131, 209, 872, 1278, 2193) |
| 1<sup>r</sup> | This manuscript was re-discovered in 1861 by F. Delitzsch and a critical account of it published by him (illustrated by a facsimile) in the first part of his *Handschriftliche Funde* (Leipzig, 1861). Tregelles also, in the second part of the same work, published an independent collation of his own (with 'Notes' prefixed), which he had made at Erlangen in 1862 (Leipzig, 1862) |
| | H. Achelis, *Hippolytstudien*, *T & U* I 4 (Leipzig, 1897), pp. 231–3 |
| | Georg Grupp, *Öttingen-Wallersteinische Sammlungen in Maihingen. Handschriften-Verzeichnis* I (Nördlingen, 1897) |
| | Hoskier, *Text* 1, pp. 7–12 |
| 2<sup>e</sup> | C.C. Tarelli, 'Erasmus's Manuscripts of the Gospels', *JTS* XLIV (1943), 155–62 |
| | K.W. Clark, 'Observations on the Erasmian Notes in Codex 2', in *Studia evangelica*, ed. F.L. Cross, K. Aland, *et al.*, *T & U* 73 (Berlin, 1959), pp. 749–56 |
| Plates | A & A 2 |
| | H.C. Hoskier, *A Full Account and Collation of the Greek Cursive Codex Evangelium 604* (London, 1890), appendix F |
| | von Dobschütz 12 |
| | Metzger, *Text*, 15 |
| Plates* | |
| 2<sup>ap</sup> | (See also Elliott: 1891) |

| Plates | von Dobschütz 13 |
| --- | --- |
| Plates* | |
| 3 | Collation (prepared for Wettstein) in Cambridge, Trinity College, B. XVII. 34. |

Treschow, *Tentamen Descriptionis codicum veterum aliquot Graecorum Novi Foederis manuscriptorum* (Copenhagen, 1773), pp. 85 ff.

| Plates | Hatch LI |
| --- | --- |
| Plates* | |
| 5 | Description in Turyn, *GB*, pp. 26–7 |
| Plates | Hatch XCI |
| 6 | (See 1739: Birdsall) |
| 7 | |
| Plates* | |
| 8 | |
| Plates* | |
| 9 | |
| Plates | Omont, *Facs* (1891), 48 |

Lake and Lake V, 190

| Plates* | |
| --- | --- |
| 12 | |
| Plates* | |
| 13 | T. K. Abbott, *Hermathena* I (Dublin, 1873), pp. 313–31 |

W. H. Ferrar, *A Collation of Four Important Manuscripts of the Gospels*, ed. T. K. Abbott (Dublin, 1877) (= 13, 69, 124, 346)

J. R. Harris, *On the Origin of the Ferrar Group* (Cambridge, 1893)

J. R. Harris, *Further Researches into the History of the Ferrar Group* (London, 1900)

J. P. P. Martin, *Introduction à la critique textuelle du Nouveau Testament* III (*partie pratique*) (Paris, 1885), pp. 188–206

J.P.P. Martin, *Quatre manuscripts du N.T.
auxquels on peut ajouter un cinquième* (Paris,
1886)

T.K. Abbott, 'Some New Members of the Ferrar
Group of Manuscripts of the Gospels' *JTS* I (1899),
117–20

fam. 13   B. Botte, 'Ferrar (Groupe de manuscripts de)',
*Supplément au Dictionnaire de la Bible* 3, ed. Louis
Pirot (Paris, 1938), cols. 272–4

K. and S. Lake, *Family 13 (The Ferrar Group). The
Text According to Mark with a Collation of Codex
28 of the Gospels, Studies and Documents* XI
(London, 1941)

Jacob Geerlings, *Family 13. (The Ferrar Group).
The Text According to Matthew, Studies and
Documents* XIX (Salt Lake City, 1961); id., *Family
13 (The Ferrar Group). The Text According to
Luke, Studies and Documents* XX (Salt Lake City,
1961); id., *Family 13 (The Ferrar Group). The Text
According to John, Studies and Documents* XXI
(Salt Lake City, 1962)

J. Geerlings, 'Family 13 and EFGH', appendix A
of *Studies and Documents* XIX (see above)

13

Plates   A & A 41

J.P.P. Martin, *Introduction à la critique textuelle
du Nouveau Testament* (Paris, 1884–6), V, plates
XXX and XXXI

J. Geerlings, *Family 13 in John, S & D* XXI, plate I

Hatch LXVII

Plates*

(see also 250: Birdsall)

Family 13   See also 69, 88, 124, 174, 230, 346, 543, 788, 826,
828, 983, 1689, 1709)

14

Plates   B. de Montfaucon, *Palaeographia Graeca* (Paris,
1708), p.282, no. V

|  | J.B. Silvestre, *Paléographie universelle* (Paris, 1841), II |
|  | Hatch X |
| Plates* | |
| 15 | |
| Plates* | |
| 16 | |
| Plates* | |
| 17 | |
| Plates | Hatch XCV |
| 18 | Hoskier, *Text* 1, pp. 150–7 (for r) |
| 19 | |
| Plates* | |
| 21 | |
| Plates* | |
| 22 | Henry A. Sanders, 'A New Collation of MS 22 of the Gospels', *JBL* 33 (1914), 91–117 |
| Plates | Hatch XLV |
| Plates* | |
| (22 | See fam 1) |
| 24 | |
| Plates | Hatch XXXVII |
| Plates* | |
| 26 | |
| Plates | Hatch XLVIII |
| 27 | |
| Plates | Hatch XX |
| Plates* | |
| 28 | |
| Plates | Hatch XL |
| Plates* | |
| (28 | See 13 (Lake)) |

| | |
|---|---|
| **29** | |
| Plates | Hatch XXIX |
| Plates* | |
| **31** | |
| Plates* | |
| **32** | |
| Plates | Hatch LVII |
| **33** | Collated by S.P. Tregelles and used in his edition of the Latin and Greek New Testament (London, 1857–79) |
| Plates | Hatch III |
| | Scrivener, *Intr*, 4th edn, I, plate XIII, no. 39 |
| | A & A 42 |
| **34** | |
| Plates | Hatch IX |
| Plates* | |
| **35** | Hoskier, *Text* 1, pp. 32–3 (for r) |
| | (See also Elliott: 322) |
| Plates | Hatch XXXIV |
| **36** | T.K. Abbott, *Hermathena* 10 (1882), 151–3 (and facsimiles) |
| Plates | Hatch XIV |
| | A & A 43 |
| Plates* | |
| **38** | Berger de Xivrey, *Notice d'un ms grec du XIII$^e$ siècle conservé à la bibliothèque impériale* ... (Paris, 1863) (in *Bibliothèque de l'école des chartes* 24, vol. 4 (Paris, 1863), pp. 97–118) |
| Plates | Colwell, *Four Gospels*, plates VI, IX |
| Plates* | |
| **40** | |
| Plates | Hatch XLVI |
| **42** | Collations by: Heinrich Middeldorf, *Biblischexeget. Repert.*, ed. E.F.K. und G.H. Rosenmüller, vol. 2 (Leipzig, 1824), pp. 87–118, and by E.F.K. |

|        | Rosenmüller, *Commentatt. theol.* vol.2, pt 2 (Leipzig, 1832), pp.167–206 |
|        | Hoskier, *Text* 1, pp.25–7 (for r) |
| (44    | See 07 (fam. E)) |
| 44     | |
| Plates | Hatch LXIII |
| 45     | |
| Plates | Hatch LVIII |
| Plates* | |
| 46     | |
| Plates* | |
| 48     | |
| Plates | Hatch LXVI |
| 49     | |
| Plates | Hatch LV |
| 50     | |
| Plates | Hatch XXXVI |
| 50     | |
| Plates | Hutter, plate 147 |
| Plates* | |
| 51     | F. Delitzsch, *Studien zur Entstehungsgeschichte der Polyglottenbibel des Cardinal Ximines* (Leipzig, 1871) |
| 52     | |
| Plates | Turyn, *GB*, 27: description pp.44ff. |
| Plates* | |
| 53     | |
| Plates | Hatch LXXXII |
| 54     | |
| Plates | Wilson and Stefanović 2 |
| (56    | See 61 (Dobbin)) |
| (58    | See 61 (Dobbin)) |
| 59     | Scrivener, *Adversaria* (as c) |

| | |
|---|---|
| Plates* | |
| 60 | Hoskier, *Text*, 1, p.16 (for r) |
| Plates | Turyn, *GB*, 45; description p.66 |
| 61 | Orlando T. Dobbin, *The Codex Montfortianus, a Collation of this Celebrated MS ... throughout the Gospels and Acts with the Greek Text of Wetstein and with certain MSS (Evv 56, 58, Ag 33) in the University of Oxford* (London, 1854) |
| | P.J. Bruns, in *Repert f Bibl und Morgenl Liter* 3 (Leipzig, 1778), pp.258ff. |
| | Hoskier, *Text* 1, pp.289–92 (for r) |
| 63 | |
| Plates* | |
| (65 | See 07 (fam. E)) |
| 66 | Scrivener, *Adversaria* (as d) |
| Plates | Hatch LXXXVI |
| 67 | |
| Plates | Hatch XLI |
| Plates* | |
| 69 | W.H. Ferrar, *A Collation of Four Important Manuscripts of the Gospels*, ed. T.K. Abbott (Dublin, 1877), and plate |
| | J. Rendel Harris, *The Origin of the Leicester Codex of the New Testament* (London, 1887) (with reproduction of one page) |
| | Scrivener, *Transcript*, pp.40–7, (as L) |
| | M.R. James, 'The Scribe of the Leicester Codex', *JTS* V (1904), 445–7, and 1 plate (see also *JTS* XI (1910), 291–2 and *JTS* XII (1911), 465–6) |
| | Hoskier, *Text* 1, pp.27 and 289–92 (for r) |
| | (see also J.N. Birdsall, *Classical Review* XXXIII (Oxford, 1983), 304, 306) |
| Plates | *Metzger, Manuscripts* 45 |
| | Scrivener, *Exact Transcript*, opp. p.xl. |
| | Scrivener, *Intr.*, 4th edn, I, plate XIII (40) |

|  | Plate II in J. Geerlings, *Family 13 in John, S & D* XXI |
|---|---|
|  | Hatch XCIV |
| Plates* |  |
| (69 | See fam. 13) |
| 71 | Scrivener, *Full and Exact Collation*, XXXVI (as g) |
| Plates | New Pal Soc I, 5 |
| 72 | J. W. Burgon, *The Last Twelve Verses of the Gospel According to St. Mark* (Oxford/London, 1871) |
| Plates | Vogels 15 |
| Plates* |  |
| 75 | Discussion and partial collation in H. C. Hoskier, *A Full Account and Collation of the Greek Cursive Codex Evangelium 604* (London, 1890), appendix G |
| Plates* |  |
| 76 |  |
| Plates* |  |
| 77 |  |
| Plates | Hatch XXXV |
| Plates* |  |
| 81 | Scrivener, *Exact Transcript*, pp. 68−70 (as p) |
|  | Collation of Acts in Tischendorf, *Anecdota* (the only cursive he seems to have examined!) |
| Plates | Lake & Lake II, 70 |
|  | New Pal Soc I, 179 |
|  | Kenyon (1912), IX |
| 82 | Hoskier, *Text* 1, p. 13 (for r) |
| Plates | Hatch XI |
| 83 |  |
| Plates | Hatch XXXI |
| 87 | Balthasar Cordier, *Catena patrum Graecorum in s. Joannem ex antiquissimo Graeco codice MS. nunc primum in luce edita* (Antwerp, 1630) |

| | |
|---|---|
| 88 | Ernst von Dobschütz, 'A hitherto unpublished Prologue to the Acts of the Apostles', *AJT* 2 (1898), 353–87 |
| | H.S. Murphy, 'On the Text of Codices H and 93', *JBL* 78 (1959), 228–37 and 1 plate (and 015), id., 'The Text of Romans and I Corinthians in Minuscule 93 and the Text of Pamphilius', *HTR* LII 2 (1959), 119–31 (n.b. 93p = 88) |
| | Hoskier, *Text* 1, pp.298–300 (for r) |
| (88 | See fam. 13) |
| 89 | Matthaei (as 20) |
| 91 | Hoskier, *Text* 1, p.13 (for r) |
| Plates* | |
| 92 | |
| Plates | Hatch XXVIII |
| Plates* | |
| 93 | Hoskier, *Text* 1, p.37 (for r) |
| 94 | H.C. Hoskier, 'Manuscripts of the Apocalypse – Recent Investigations V', *BJRL* vol.8 pt2 (1924), 13–16 |
| | Hoskier, *Text* 1, pp.34–6 (for r) |
| 98 | |
| Plates | Hatch XLVII |
| Plates* | |
| (98 | See 07 (fam. E)) |
| 99 | Matthaei (as 18) |
| Plates | Hatch XCVII |
| 100 | S. Márkfi, *Codex Graecus Quattuor Evangeliorum e Bibliotheca Universitatis Pestinensis* (Pest, 1860) |
| Plates | Hatch XIII |
| 101 | Matthaei (as a) |
| 102 | Matthaei (as c) |
| Plates* | |
| 103 | Treu, pp.288–91 |
| | Matthaei (as d) |

| 104 | Hoskier, *Text* 1, p. 14 (for r) |
| | Scrivener, *Exact Transcript*, p. 76 (as 1) |
| Plates | New Pal Soc I, 179 |
| | Lake and Lake II, 73 |
| Plates* | |
| 105 | |
| Plates* | |
| 106 | R. P. Casey, 'The "Lost" Codex 106 of the Gospels', *HTR* 16 (1923), 394−6 |
| | Treu, pp. 339−41 |
| 107 | |
| Plates* | |
| 108 | |
| Plates* | |
| 109 | |
| Plates | Turyn, *GB*, pp. 61−8; description pp. 94 f. |
| 110 | Scrivener, *Exact Transcript*, pp. 71−2 (as d) |
| | Hoskier, *Text* 1, p. 14 (for r) |
| 111 | Colwell, *Four Gospels*, I, pp. 170−222 |
| 112 | |
| Plates* | |
| 113 | |
| Plates* | |
| 115 | |
| Plates | Hatch XXIII |
| Plates* | |
| 117 | |
| Plates | Hatch XCII |
| 118 | |
| Plates | Hatch LXXIV |
| (118 | See fam. 1) |
| 119 | |
| Plates | Hatch LXII |

| | |
|---|---|
| 120 | Colwell, *Four Gospels*, I, pp. 170–222 |
| Plates* | |
| 123 | |
| Plates* | |
| 124 | W. H. Ferrar, *A Collation of Four Important Manuscripts of the Gospels*, ed. T. K. Abbott (Dublin, 1877) |
| | J. Rendel Harris, *On the Origin of the Ferrar Group* (Cambridge, 1893); id., *Further Researches into the History of the Ferrar Group* (London, 1900) |
| | E. A. Hutton, 'Excursus on the Ferrar Group', in *An Atlas of Textual Criticism* (Cambridge, 1911), pp. 49–53 |
| | Jacob Geerlings, 'Singular Variants in 124' = Appendix A of Jacob Geerlings, *Family 13 in Mt*, *S & D* XX, pp. 149–52 |
| | Jacob Geerlings, 'Singular Variants in Codex 124 (in Jn)' = appendix B of J. Geerlings, *Family 13 in John*, *S & D* XXI, pp. 108–11 |
| Plates | T. K. Abbott, *A Collation of Four Important Manuscripts of the Gospels* (Dublin, 1877), ad init. |
| | Hatch XXII |
| | Metzger, *Manuscripts*, 36 |
| Plates* | |
| (124 | See fam. 13) |
| 125 | |
| Plates* | |
| 126 | |
| Plates | *Handschriften und Aldinen* (Wolfenbüttel, 1978), plate 9 (library exhibition catalogue) |
| 128 | |
| Plates | Hatch LXXVII |
| 129 | |
| Plates* | |

| 131 | |
|-----|---|
| Plates | Hatch LXXXVII |
| (131 | See fam. 1) |
| 132 | |
| Plates | Hatch LXIX |
| Plates* | |
| 134 | |
| Plates* | |
| 135 | |
| Plates | Hatch XXVII |
| Plates | Hatch XLIII |
| 137 | |
| Plates* | |
| 139 | |
| Plates | Lake and Lake VIII, 321 |
| 140 | |
| Plates* | |
| 141 | H.C. Hoskier, 'Manuscripts of the Apocalypse – Recent Investigations V', *BJRL* vol. 8, pt 2 (1924), 16–17 |
| | Hoskier, *Text* 1, pp. 104–7 (for r) |
| 143 | |
| Plates* | |
| 144 | |
| Plates | Hatch XII |
| 147 | |
| Plates | Hatch LXXVIII |
| 149 | Hoskier, *Text* 1, pp. 53–5 (for r) |
| Plates | Hatch XCIII |
| 151 | |
| Plates | Hatch XIX |
| Plates* | |
| 152 | |
| Plates | Hatch LXXIII |

| | |
|---|---|
| 153 | |
| Plates | Hatch LXXXIII |
| 155 | H.J. de Jonge, 'The Manuscriptus Evangeliorum Antiquissimus of Daniel Hensius', *NTS* 21 (1974–5), 286–94 |
| Plates | Hatch LXXXIV |
| 57 | Collated by H.C. Hoskier, 'Evan. 157', *JTS* XIV (1913), 78–116, 242–93, 359–84 |
| | B.H. Streeter, 'Codices 157, 1071 and the Caesarean Text', in Lake F/S, pp. 149–50 |
| Plates | New Pal Soc I, 106 |
| | Lake and Lake VIII, 313 |
| Plates* | |
| 159 | |
| Plates | Lake and Lake VIII, 308 |
| 160 | |
| Plates | Lake and Lake VIII, 309 |
| 161 | |
| Plates | Hatch XVI |
| 162 | |
| Plates | Lake and Lake VIII, 317 |
| Plates* | |
| 163 | |
| Plates | Lake and Lake VIII, 328 |
| Plates* | |
| 164 | |
| Plates | Lake and Lake VII, 285 and IX, 340 |
| Plates* | |
| 165 | V. Gardthausen, in *Sitzungsbericht der phil.-hist. Classe der sächs. Gesellschaft der Wissenschaften* 32 (Leipzig, 1880), pp. 73–8 |
| | (For other manuscripts written in Calabria, see Robert Devreesse, *Les Manuscrits grecs de l'Italie méridionale, Studi e Testi* 183 (Vatican City, 1955), pp. 37–43; see also M.-L. Concasty, 'Manuscrits grecs originaires de l'Italie méridionale conservés à |

Paris', in *Atti dello VIII Congresso Internazionale
di studi bizantini* I, *Studi Bizantini e Neoellenici*
VII (1953), p. 29 n. 1, and Paul Canart, 'Le
Problème du style d'écriture dit "en as de pique"
dans manuscrits italo-grecs', *Atti del IV Congresso
Storico Calabrese* (Naples, 1969) pp. 53–69)

| | |
|---|---|
| Plates | Metzger, *Manuscripts*, 40 |
| | Turyn (1964), plate 47; description pp. 78–86 |
| | Cavalieri and Lietzmann, 38 |
| Plates* | |
| 167 | V. Puntoni, in *Studi italiani di filologia classica* 3 (Florence, 1895), p. 495 |
| 169 | |
| Plates* | |
| 172 | Hoskier, *Text* 1, p. 275 (for r) |
| | Scrivener, *Exact Transcript*, pp. 76–7 (as m) |
| 174 | |
| Plates | Lake and Lake VII, 287 |
| | Barbour 21 |
| | Plate III in J. Geerlings, *Family E in John*, S & D XXI |
| (174 | See fam. 13) |
| 175 | Hoskier, *Text* 1, p. 38 (for r) |
| 177 | Acts collated by F. Delitzsch, *Handschriftliche Funde* 2 (Leipzig, 1862), pp. 45–8 |
| | Hoskier, *Text* 1, pp. 271f. (for r) |
| 178 | |
| Plates* | |
| 180 | Hoskier, *Text* 1, pp. 117–20 (for r) |
| Plates | Turyn, *Vatican*, 29, 30, 31; description p. 50 |
| | Follieri 51 |
| Plates* | |
| 181 | Hoskier, *Text* 1, pp. 17–24 (for r) |
| 186 | |
| Plates* | |

| | |
|---|---|
| 187 | |
| Plates* | |
| 190 | |
| Plates* | |
| 197 | |
| Plates* | |
| 199 | |
| Plates* | |
| 200 | |
| Plates* | |
| 201 | Hoskier, *Text* 1, p. 293 (for r) |
| | Scrivener, *Exact Transcript*, p. 63 (as h) |
| | Scrivener, *Full and Exact Collation*, p. xliv (as m) |
| 203 | Hoskier, *Text* 1, pp. 338–41 (for r) |
| Plates | Lake and Lake II, 77 |
| | Pal Soc I, 84 |
| Plates* | |
| 205 | Hoskier, *Text* 1, p. 307 (for r) |
| 205 | |
| Plates* | |
| 206 | Scrivener, *Exact Transcript*, pp. 55–7 (as a) |
| | V. Davey, *A Study of the New Testament Manuscripts 206 and 429 in the Pauline and Catholic Epistles*, Unpublished M.A. Thesis, University of Birmingham, 1970 |
| 207 | L. Politis, *Paléographie et littérature byzantine et néo-grecque* VI (1975), p. 23 |
| Plates | Furlan I, 43 and 44 |
| | T. Gasparrini Leporace and E. Mioni, *Cento Codici Bessarionei* (Venice, 1968), table 11 (exhibition catalogue) |
| | (See also Elliott: 1891) |
| 209 | Hoskier, *Text* 1, pp. 127–32 (for r) |
| (209 | See fam. 1) |

212
Plates*

213 J.N. Birdsall, 'The Missing Leaves of Codex 213 of the New Testament', *JTS* IX (1958), 78–81

215
Plates*

216 Scrivener, *Exact Transcript*, pp. 57–8 (as b)
(See also Elliott: 322)

217
Plates*

218 F.C. Alter, *Novum Testamentum ad Codicum Vindobonensem Graece expressum* (Vienna, 1786–7)
Hoskier, *Text* 1, pp. 68–9 (for r)

Plates Hatch LXXV
Plates*

(219 See 07 (fam. E))

219

Plates Hatch LXXII

220
Plates*

221
Plates*

223 Scrivener, *Adversaria* (as a)
In K.W. Clark, *Eight American Praxapostoloi* (Chicago, 1941)
Clark, *USA*, pp. 312–13

Plates Metzger, *Manuscripts*, 43
Clark 51

224
Plates*

225

Plates Lake and Lake IX, 360
Plates*

226

Plates          Graux and Martin, plate 10 and facs. 33−7

Plates*

229

Plates*

230             J. Geerlings' collation of 230 in Mark = Appendix
                A of J. Geerlings, *Family 13 in John*, *S & D* XXI,
                pp. 101−7

                Collation of 230 in Matthew = Appendix B of J.
                Geerlings, *Family 13 in Luke*, *S & D* XX,
                pp. 153−5

Plates          Plate IV in J. Geerlings, *Family 13 in John*, *S & D*
                XXI

Plates*

(230            See fam. 13)

232             Collation by Matthaei (as 10)

236             J. R. Harris, 'On a New Ms of the Four Gospels',
                *Haverford College Studies* 4 (1890), 22−7 (partial
                collation)

237             Treu, pp. 266−7

                Matthaei (as d)

238             Matthaei (as e and as 11)

                Treu, pp. 276−7

                H. Gebhardt, 'Untersuchungen zu der
                Evangelienhandschrift 238', *ZNW* 7 (1906), 120−2

239             Matthaei (as g)

                Treu, pp. 264−5

240             Matthaei (as i)

                Treu, pp. 270−2

Plates          von Dobschütz, 17

Plates*

241             Hoskier, *Text* 1, pp. 133−7 (for r)

                Matthaei (as k)

242             Matthaei (as l)

|          | Hoskier, *Text* 1, pp. 138–41 (for r) |
|----------|---------------------------------------|
|          | Treu, pp. 258–60                      |
| Plates*  |                                       |
| 243      | Matthaei (as m)                       |
|          | Treu, pp. 278–80                      |
| 244      | Matthaei (as n)                       |
|          | Treu, pp. 272–4                       |
| 245      | Matthaei (as o)                       |
| Plates   | Cereteli and Sobolewski I, 24         |
|          | Lake and Lake VI, 233                 |
| Plates*  |                                       |
| 246      | Matthaei (as p)                       |
|          | Treu, pp. 249–51                      |
| 247      | Matthaei (as q)                       |
|          | Treu, pp. 244–6                       |
| 248      | Matthaei (as r)                       |
|          | Treu, pp. 246–9                       |
| Plates   | Cereteli and Sobolewski I, 25         |
| Plates*  |                                       |
| 249      | Matthaei (as s)                       |
|          | Treu, pp. 274–5                       |
| Plates*  |                                       |
| 250      | J.N. Birdsall, 'A Byzantine Calendar from the Menology of two Biblical Mss.', *Anal Boll* 84 (1966), 29–57 |
|          | (see also 13, 424, *l* 547, *l* 1748) |
|          | Matthaei (as v)                       |
|          | Hoskier, *Text* 1, pp. 556ff. (for r) |
| 251      | Matthaei (as x)                       |
|          | Treu, pp. 311–13                      |
| 252      | Matthaei (as z)                       |
| 253      | Matthaei (as 10)                      |
|          | Treu, pp. 360–7                       |

| | |
|---|---|
| 254 | Hoskier, *Text* 1, pp. 747–51 (for r) |
| | Matthaei (as 11) |
| 255 | Matthaei (as 12) |
| 256 | Matthaei (as 13 and 14) |
| | Hoskier, *Text* 1, pp. 347–52 (for r) |
| Plates* | |
| 258 | Matthaei (as 17) |
| 259 | Matthaei (as a) |
| | Treu, pp. 268–70 |
| 260 | |
| Plates* | |
| 262 | |
| Plates | Hatch XVII |
| Plates* | |
| (265 | See 041: fam. Π) |
| 267 | |
| Plates* | |
| 269 | 2 plates in I. Spatharakis, *The Portrait in Byzantine Illustrated Manuscripts*, *Byzantina Neerlandica* 6 (Leiden, 1976) |
| | Paintings in: H. Omont, *Évangiles avec peintures*, 2 (Paris, 1908) |
| Plates* | |
| 270 | |
| Plates* | |
| 271 | |
| Plates* | |
| 274 | |
| Plates | Hatch XVIII |
| | von Dobschütz 20 |
| | Metzger, *Text*, 11 |
| Plates* | |

| | |
|---|---|
| 276 | |
| Plates | Omont, *Facs* (1891), 39 |
| | Lake and Lake V, 180 |
| Plates* | |
| 282 | |
| Plates | Omont, *Facs* (1891), 49 |
| | Lake and Lake V, 191 |
| Plates* | |
| 284 | |
| Plates* | |
| 289 | |
| Plates* | |
| 293 | |
| Plates | Omont, *Facs* (1891), 56 |
| Plates* | |
| 294 | |
| Plates | Omont, *Facs* (1891), 66 |
| Plates* | |
| 296 | Hoskier, *Text* 1, pp. 174–80 (for r) |
| | (See also Elliott: 1891) |
| 298 | |
| Plates* | |
| 300 | |
| Plates* | |
| 303 | |
| Plates | Omont, *Facs* (1891), 54 |
| Plates* | |
| 314 | Hoskier, *Text* 1, p. 14 (for r) |
| Plates* | |
| 319 | Scrivener, *Exact Transcript*, pp. 64–6 (as l) |
| 322 | W. J. Elliott, 'The Relationship between 322 and 323 of the Greek New Testament', *NTS* 14 (1968), 271–81 |

|         |                                                                                                                                                                              |
|---------|------------------------------------------------------------------------------------------------------------------------------------------------------------------------------|
|         | W. J. Elliott, *An Examination of von Soden's I b2 Group of MSS*, Unpublished M.A. thesis, University of Birmingham, 1969 (Collations of 1739, 2298, 323, 322, 440, 216, 1872, 1149, 491, 35, 935) |
| Plates  | A & A 44                                                                                                                                                                      |
| 323     | W. J. Elliott, 'The Relationship between 322 and 323 of the Greek New Testament', *NTS* 14 (1968), 271–81                                                                     |
| Plates  | A & A 44                                                                                                                                                                      |
|         | (See also Elliott 322)                                                                                                                                                        |
| 325     | Hoskier, *Text* 1, p. 15 (for r)                                                                                                                                              |
| 326     | Acts portions collated by O. T. Dobbin, *The Codex Montfortianus* (London, 1854)                                                                                              |
| 330     | Collation in Muralt, *NT Gr* 1848                                                                                                                                             |
|         | Colwell, *Four Gospels*, I, pp. 170–222                                                                                                                                       |
|         | Treu, 63–7                                                                                                                                                                    |
|         | (New collation by M. Davies (see 2344))                                                                                                                                       |
| Plates* |                                                                                                                                                                              |
| 331     |                                                                                                                                                                              |
| Plates  | Hatch XXV                                                                                                                                                                     |
|         | Pal Soc I, 204                                                                                                                                                                |
| 336     | Hoskier, *Text* 1, pp. 26–7 (for r)                                                                                                                                           |
| 337     | Hoskier, *Text* 1, pp. 158–61 (for r)                                                                                                                                         |
| 338     | W. Reader, 'Entdeckung von Fragmenten aus zwei zerstörten Minuskeln (338 und 612)', *Biblica* 61, (1980) 407–11 (see also 612)                                               |
| 339     | G. de Sanctis, *Rivista di Filologiae d'Istruzione Classica* 32 (1904), 584                                                                                                   |
| 343     |                                                                                                                                                                              |
| Plates* |                                                                                                                                                                              |
| 346     | Collation by W. H. Ferrar, *A Collation of Four Important mss. of the Gospels*, ed. T. K. Abbott (Dublin, 1877)                                                               |
| Plates  | Plate V in J. Geerlings, *Family 13 in John*, S & D XXI                                                                                                                       |

| Plates* | |
|---|---|
| (346 | See fam. 13) |
| 348 | |
| Plates | Lake and Lake III, 126 |
| | Pal Soc I, 130 |
| Plates* | |
| 349 | |
| Plates | Turyn (1972), 122, 123, 124; description p. 147 |
| 350 | |
| Plates* | |
| 355 | |
| Plates* | |
| 356 | Scrivener, *Exact Transcript*, pp. 66–8 (as n) and 1 facsimile |
| 364 | |
| Plates* | |
| 365 | |
| Plates* | |
| 367 | Hoskier, *Text* 1, pp. 47–50 (for r) |
| Plates* | |
| 368 | Hoskier, *Text* 1, pp. 273–5 (for r) |
| 371 | |
| Plates | Hatch XXVI |
| 372 | |
| Plates | Hatch XCVI |
| 374 | |
| Plates | Lake and Lake IX, 336 |
| 379 | |
| Plates* | |
| 380 | |
| Plates | D. Harlfinger, *Specimina griechischer Kopisten der Renaissance* I (Berlin, 1974), 78 |

| | |
|---|---|
| 383 | Readings from Acts in A. Pott, *Der abendländische Text der Apostelgeschichte und die Wir-quelle* (Leipzig, 1900), pp. 78–88 |
| | A. V. Valentine-Richards, *The Text of Acts in Codex 614 (Tisch 137) and its Allies* (Cambridge, 1934) |
| 385 | Scrivener, *Exact Transcript*, p. 72 (as e) |
| | Hoskier, *Text* 1, p. 55 (for r) |
| 386 | Hoskier, *Text* 1, pp. 227 f. |
| 389 | |
| Plates | Hatch XLII |
| 390 | |
| Plates | Turyn (1964) 37; description pp. 65 ff. |
| | Cavalieri and Lietzmann 32 |
| 394 | |
| Plates | Turyn (1972), 141: description pp. 175 f. |
| Plates* | |
| 395 | |
| Plates* | |
| 399 | Treu, pp. 88–90 |
| 406 | J. N. Birdsall, '406, A Neglected Witness to the Caesarean Text', in *Studia evangelica*, ed. K. Aland, F. L. Cross *et al.*, *T & U* 73 (Berlin, 1959), pp. 732–6 |
| 409 | |
| Plates* | |
| 410 | |
| Plates* | |
| 411 | |
| Plates* | |
| 412 | |
| Plates | Turyn (1972) 79; description pp. 100 f. |
| Plates* | |
| 413 | |
| Plates* | |

| | |
|---|---|
| 414 | |
| Plates* | |
| 415 | |
| Plates | Turyn (1972) 174; description pp. 216f. |
| Plates* | |
| 421 | |
| Plates | Bick 18; description p. 31 |
| | Hatch LIV |
| Plates | |
| (422 | See 07 (fam. E)) |
| 424 | Hoskier, *Text* 1, pp. 70–3 (for r) |
| | J. N. Birdsall, 'A Byzantine Calendar from the Menology of two Biblical Mss', *Anal Boll* 84 (1966), 29–57 (see also 13, 250, *l* 547, *l* 1748) |
| (424 | See 1739 (Birdsall)) |
| Plates | A & A 45 |
| Plates* | |
| 425 | |
| Plates | Bick 22; description p. 35 |
| Plates* | |
| 427 | |
| Plates | Hatch LXXVI |
| 428 | |
| Plates* | |
| 429 | Matthaei (as x) |
| | Hoskier, *Text* I, pp. 56–62 (for r) |
| | (see also Elliott: 1891 and Davey: 206) |
| 431 | J. Valentine-Richards, 'Hilgenfeld's Edition of the Acts', *JTS* I, 606–13 and see also id., *The Text of Acts in Codex 614 (Tisch. 137) and its Allies* (Cambridge, 1934), appendix I |
| 432 | Hoskier, *Text* 1, pp. 85–9 (for r) |
| (436 | New Collation by M. Davies (see 2344)) |

| 438 | |
|---|---|
| Plates | Pattie 10 |
| Plates* | |
| 439 | |
| Plates | Lake and Lake II, 81 |
| 440 | Scrivener, *Exact Transcript*, pp. 35–8 (as v) |
| | (See also Elliott: 322) |
| 441 & 442 | Ed. P.F. Aurivill, *Codex Graecus Nov. Foederis* (Uppsala, 1783, 1786) |
| 443 | |
| Plates | Hatch LVI |
| 444 | |
| Plates | Hatch LXXXVIII |
| 445 | |
| Plates* | |
| 447 | |
| Plates | Hatch LXXXIX |
| 448 | |
| Plates* | |
| 450 | |
| Plates* | |
| 452 | Hoskier, *Text* 1, pp. 110–14 (for r) |
| Plates* | |
| 454 | |
| Plates | Vogels 16 |
| 456 | Hoskier, *Text* 1, pp. 240–5 (for r) |
| Plates | Vogels 13 |
| Plates* | |
| 459 | Hoskier, *Text* 1, pp. 121–6 (for r) |
| Plates | Lake and Lake X, 373 |
| 461 | G. Cereteli, 'Wo ist das Tetraevangelium von Porphyrius Uspenskij aus dem Jahr 835 erstanden?', *Byz Z* IX (1900), 649–53. |
| | T.W. Allen, 'The Origin of the Greek Minuscule Hand', *JHS* XL (1920), 1–12 |

|         |                                                                                                      |
| ------- | ---------------------------------------------------------------------------------------------------- |
|         | A. Diller, 'A Companion to the Uspenski Gospels', *Byz Z* XLIX (1956), 332–5                          |
|         | Treu, pp. 84–7                                                                                        |
| Plates  | Lake and Lake VI, 234                                                                                 |
|         | Cereteli and Sobolewski II, plates 1 and 1a                                                           |
|         | Barbour 12 and 13                                                                                     |
|         | Hatch I                                                                                               |
|         | Metzger, *Manuscripts*, 26                                                                            |
|         | Lefort and Cochez 4                                                                                   |
|         | A & A 46 and 47                                                                                        |
|         | W. Wattenbach and A. von Velsen, *Exempla codicum Graecorum litteris minusculis scriptorum* (Heidelberg, 1878), plate 1 |
| 462     | Matthaei (as f)                                                                                       |
|         | Treu, pp. 254–8                                                                                       |
| (462    | New collation by M. Davies (See 2344))                                                                |
| 463     | Matthaei (as h)                                                                                       |
|         | Treu, pp. 285–8                                                                                       |
| 464     | Matthaei (as m)                                                                                       |
|         | Treu, pp. 251–4                                                                                       |
| 467     | Hoskier, *Text* 1, pp. 162–5 (for r)                                                                  |
| 468     | Hoskier, *Text* 1, pp. 166–9 (for r)                                                                  |
| 469     | Hoskier, *Text* 1, pp. 170–8 (for r)                                                                  |
| 470     | Scrivener, *Full and Exact Collation*, p. xxvi (as a)                                                 |
| 471     | Scrivener, *Full and Exact Collation*, p. xxvii (as b)                                                |
| 472     | Scrivener, *Full and Exact Collation*, p. xxix (as c)                                                 |
| 473     | Scrivener, *Full and Exact Collation*, p. xxxi (as d)                                                 |
| Plates  | Hatch XXXII                                                                                           |
| 474     | Scrivener, *Full and Exact Collation*, p. xxxiii (as e)                                               |
| 475     | Scrivener, *Full and Exact Collation*, p. xxxiv (as f)                                                |
| 476     | Scrivener, *Full and Exact Collation*, p. xxxviii (as h)                                              |
| 477     | Scrivener, *Full and Exact Collation*, p. xxxiii (as i)                                               |
|         | Scrivener, *Exact Transcript*, pp. 33–5 (as i)                                                        |

| | |
|---|---|
| 478 | Scrivener, *Full and Exact Collation*, p. xl (as k) |
| Plates | Hatch VIII |
| | Pattie 14 |
| | *Catalogue of Ancient Manuscripts in the British Museum* (London, 1881), pt I, Greek, plate 16 |
| | E. M. Thompson, *An Introduction to Greek and Latin Palaeography* (Oxford, 1912), p. 226 |
| Plates* | |
| 479 | Scrivener, *Full and Exact Collation*, p. xlii (as l) |
| | Scrivener, *Exact Transcript*, p. 63 (as g) |
| | J. N. Birdsall, 'Greek Hagiographical Mss. in the Library of the Selly Oak Colleges', *Anal Boll* 86 (1968), 333–6 |
| Plates | Hatch LXVIII |
| 480 | |
| Plates | New Pal Soc I, 180 |
| | Scrivener, *Exact Transcript*, p. 63 (as j) |
| | Scrivener, *Full and Exact Collation*, p. xlvi (as n) |
| | Turyn, *GB*, 133; description p. 90 |
| Plates* | |
| 481 | Scrivener, *Full and Exact Collation*, p. xlviii (as o) |
| Plates | F. C. Kenyon, *Facsimiles of Biblical Manuscripts in the British Museum* (London, 1900), VI |
| | Hatch XXIV |
| Plates* | |
| 482 | Scrivener, *Full and Exact Collation*, p. xlix (as p) |
| Plates | Turyn, *GB*, 26; description pp. 42 ff. |
| Plates* | |
| 483 | Scrivener, *Exact Transcript*, p. 63 (as f) |
| | Scrivener, *Full and Exact Collation*, p. li (as q) |
| | Clark, *USA*, pp. 17–20 |
| Plates | Clark 1 |
| | Hatch, *Sinai*, LVII |
| 484 | Scrivener, *Full and Exact Collation*, p. lii (as r) |

| | |
|---|---|
| Plates | Turyn, *GB*, 43; description p. 61 |
| Plates* | |
| 485 | Scrivener, *Full and Exact Collation*, p. liv (as s) |
| 486 | Scrivener, *Full and Exact Collation*, p. lv (as t) |
| 487 | Scrivener, *Full and Exact Collation*, p. lvii (as u) (now lost) |
| 488 | Scrivener, *Full and Exact Collation*, p. lvii (as v) |
| 489 | Scrivener, *Exact Transcript*, pp. 38–40 (as w) |
| (489 | See 041 (fam. Π)) |
| Plates | Turyn, *GB*, 55; description p. 81 |
| 490 | Collated by T. K. Abbott, *Hermathena* XVIII (1892), 233 f. |
| 491 | (See also Elliott: 322) |
| Plates* | |
| 492 | |
| Plates | Turyn, *GB*, 60; description p. 91 |
| 492 | |
| Plates | New Pal Soc I, 130 |
| 498 | Scrivener, *Exact Transcript*, p. 74 (as j) |
| | Hoskier, *Text* 1, p. 296 (for r) |
| Plates | Hatch LXXXV |
| 504 | |
| Plates | Lake and Lake II, 69 |
| | Pal Soc I, 202 |
| 506 | Scrivener, *Adversaria* (as e) |
| | Hoskier, *Text* 1, p. 55 (for r) |
| Plates | Hatch XLIV |
| Plates* | |
| 509 | |
| Plates* | |
| 510 | |
| Plates* | |

| | |
|---|---|
| 512 | |
| Plates | Hatch XC |
| 513 | |
| Plates | Lake and Lake V, 197 |
| Plates* | |
| 514 | |
| Plates | Hatch LIX |
| 516 | |
| Plates | Hatch LXIV |
| 517 | Scrivener, *Adversaria* (as f) |
| | Hoskier, *Text* 1, p. 55 (for r) |
| Plates | Hatch XXXIX |
| 521 | |
| Plates | Turyn, *GB*, 59; description p. 89 |
| 522 | Scrivener, *Exact Transcript*, pp. 75−6 (as k) |
| | Hoskier, *Text* 1, p. 297 (for r) |
| | (See also Elliott: 1891) |
| 523 | |
| Plates | Hatch LIII |
| Plates* | |
| 524 | |
| Plates* | |
| 525 | |
| Plates* | |
| 527 | |
| Plates* | |
| 528 | |
| Plates | Hatch XXXVIII |
| Plates* | |
| 529 | |
| Plates* | |
| 532 | Clark, *USA*, pp. 291−2 |
| Plates | Clark 49 |

| | |
|---|---|
| 533 | Clark, *USA*, pp. 289–91 |
| 534 | Clark, *USA*, pp. 299–300 |
| | Scrivener, *Adversaria* (as g) |
| 535 | Scrivener, *Adversaria* (as h) |
| | Clark, *USA*, pp. 288–9 |
| 536 | Scrivener, *Adversaria* (as i) |
| | Clark, *USA*, pp. 295–7 |
| Plates | Clark 50 |
| 537 | Scrivener, *Adversaria* (as k) |
| | Clark, *USA*, pp. 286–7 |
| 538 | Scrivener, *Adversaria*, (as l) |
| | Clark, *USA*, pp. 285–6 |
| | W.M. Read, *A Collation of the University of Michigan Manuscript no. 18 of the Four Gospels* (Seattle, University of Washington Press, 1942) |
| | (Review: G.D. Kilpatrick, *JTS* XLV (1944), 79) |
| 540 | Scrivener, *Adversaria* (as m) |
| | Clark, *USA*, pp. 293–4 |
| 541 | Scrivener, *Adversaria* (as n) |
| | Clark, *USA*, pp. 294–5 |
| 542 | Scrivener, *Adversaria* (as o) |
| 543 | Scrivener, *Adversaria*, (as a) |
| | Clark, *USA*, pp. 280–2 |
| | Jacob Geerlings, 'Codex 543, University of Michigan 15 (Greg. 543; von Soden ε 257)', in *Six Collations*, pp. 26–76 and plate II |
| Plates | Clark 47 |
| | Plate I of J. Geerlings, *Family 13 in Matthew*, *S & D* XIX |
| (543 | See fam. 13) |
| 544 | Scrivener, *Adversaria* (as p) |
| | Clark, *USA*, pp. 297–8 |
| | Colwell, *Four Gospels*, I, pp. 9, 204 ff. |

| | |
|---|---|
| 545 | Scrivener, *Adversaria* (as q) |
| | Clark, *USA*, pp. 305−8 |
| 546 | Scrivener, *Adversaria* (as r) |
| | Clark, *USA*, pp. 300−2 |
| 548 | |
| Plates | New Pal Soc II, 79 |
| 548 | |
| Plates* | |
| 552 | |
| Plates* | |
| 554 | |
| Plates | Turyn, *GB*, 8, 9, 10; description pp. 21 f. |
| 555 | |
| Plates | Hatch XCVIII |
| 559 | C. Steenbuch, 'Minuscule MS Evan. 559 (xi Cent.)', *JTS* XVI (1915), 264−7 |
| 561 | |
| Plates | Hatch LXXI |
| 562 | |
| Plates | Hatch C |
| 564 | |
| Plates* | |
| 565 | E. von Muralt, 'Beschreibung einer tausendjährigen prachtvollen 1829 aus Klein-Asien nach der K. Bibliothek gekommenen Handschrift der Evangelien', *Bulletin scientifique publié par l'Académie de S. Petersbourg* 4 (1835), cols. 72−80 and plate |
| | Collations in Johannes Belsheim, *Das Evangelium des Markus, Christiania Videnskabs-Selskabs Forhandlinger* 9 (Christiania, 1885) and plate (corrections to Mark in H.S. Cronin, *Texts and Studies* vol. 5, no. 4 (Cambridge, 1899), 106−8 and further corrections in I.A. Moir, *Codex Climaci rescriptus* (Cambridge, 1956), appendix 2, pp. 113−14) |

Review: A. Harnack, *TLZ* (6 March 1886)

A. Schmidtke, *Neue Fragmente und Untersuchungen zu den Evangelien*, *T & U* 37/1 (Leipzig, 1911), pp. 1–31 passim

Treu, pp. 45–8

G.D. Kilpatrick, 'Codex 565 of the Gospels', *TZ* 25 (1969), 130

| | |
|---|---|
| Plates | Hatch IV |
| Plates* | |
| 566 | Tischendorf, *Notitia*, pp. 58 ff. |
| | Treu, pp. 48–50 |
| | Schmidtke (as for 565) |
| Plates | Hatch V |
| | von Dobschütz 11 |
| | Vogels 14 |
| Plates* | |
| (566 | See also Λ (039)) |
| 568 | Treu, pp. 50–3 |
| Plates* | |
| 569 | Treu, pp. 54–7 |
| Plates | Cereteli and Sobolewski II, 17 |
| Plates* | |
| 570 | Tischendorf, *Notitia*, p. 60 |
| | Treu, pp. 57–60 |
| 571 | Collation in E. Muralt, *NT Gr* |
| | Treu, pp. 60–1 |
| Plates | Hatch XXX |
| 572 | Tischendorf, *Notitia*, p. 64 |
| | Treu, pp. 62–3 |
| 574 | Collation in E. Muralt, *NT Gr* |
| | Treu, pp. 67–70 |
| Plates | E.C. Colwell and H.R. Willoughly, *The Four Gospels of Karahissar* (2 vols., Chicago, 1936) |
| Plates* | |

| | |
|---|---|
| 575 | Treu, pp. 71–3 |
| Plates* | |
| 579 | A. Schmidtke, *Die Evangelien eines alten Unzialcodex nach einer Abschrift des dreizehnten Jahrhunderts* (Leipzig, 1903) |
| | K. Lake, 'The Ammonian Harmony and the Text of B', *JTS* VII (1906), 292–5 (reviewing Schmidtke) |
| | M.-J. Lagrange, *Critique textuelle* II, *La Critique rationelle* (Paris, 1935), pp. 113–16 |
| Plates | Hatch LXV |
| Plates* | |
| 580 | |
| Plates | Hatch L |
| 582 | Hoskier, *Text* 1, pp. 308–13 (for r) |
| 583 | |
| Plates* | |
| 585 | |
| Plates* | |
| 588 | |
| Plates | Turyn (1972), 118; description pp. 141 f. |
| 592 | |
| Plates | Turyn (1972), 45; description pp. 61 f. |
| Plates* | |
| 602 | |
| Plates | Hatch XXI |
| 605 | |
| Plates* | |
| 608 | |
| Plates* | |
| 609 | Treu, pp. 120–1 |
| Plates | Omont, *Facs* (1891), 18 |
| | Lake and Lake IV, 155 |
| (612 | See 338 (W. Reader)) |

| | |
|---|---|
| 614 | A. V. Valentine-Richards (and J. M. Creed), *The Text of Acts in Codex 614 (Tischendorf 137) and its Allies* (Cambridge, 1934) (Review by F. C. Burkitt, *JTS* XXXVI (1935), 191) |
| | *Beginnings of Christianity* III, pp. cccxvi ff. |
| Plates | A & A 48 |
| | Vogels 11 |
| 616 | Hoskier, *Text* 1, pp. 530–4 (for r) |
| 617 | Hoskier, *Text* 1, pp. 238 f. (for r) |
| 619 | |
| Plates | Lake and Lake X, 367 |
| Plates* | |
| 620 | Hoskier, *Text* 1, pp. 595 f. (for r) |
| 623 | |
| Plates | Barbour 29 |
| | Metzger, *Manuscripts*, 35 |
| | Cavalieri and Lietzmann 22 |
| | Lake and Lake VII, 283 |
| Plates* | |
| 627 | Hoskier, *Text* I, pp. 51–2 (for r) |
| 628 | Hoskier, *Text* 1, pp. 223–6 (for r) |
| 632 | Hoskier, *Text* 1, pp. 45–6 (for r) |
| 634 | |
| Plates | Barbour 59 |
| Plates* | |
| 635 | (See also Elliott: 1891) |
| 637 | |
| Plates* | |
| 642 | Scrivener, *Exact Transcript*, pp. 59–61 (as d) |
| 643 | Scrivener, *Exact Transcript*, p. 63 (as j) |
| 645 | |
| Plates | Turyn, *GB*, 46, description p. 67 |
| | Pal Soc I, 205 |
| | Barbour 70 |

| | |
|---|---|
| Plates* | |
| 653 | Treu, pp. 124–6 |
| | Beneševic II, 71 |
| Plates | Lake and Lake V, 201 |
| Plates* | |
| 659 | |
| Plates | Lake and Lake V, 202 |
| 662 | |
| Plates* | |
| 663 | |
| Plates* | |
| 664 | Hoskier, *Text* 1, pp. 330–7 (for r) |
| 666 | Description and collation in E. J. Goodspeed, 'The Harvard Gospels', *AJT* X (1906), 687–700 |
| | E. J. Goodspeed, 'The Harvard Gospels', *HLS* 6 (1919), 171–86 and 1 plate |
| | Clark, *USA*, pp. 107–9 |
| Plates | Hatch LII |
| | Finegan 22 and 23 |
| Plates* | |
| 667 | Description, Text, Analysis and Collation: Everett A. Overton, *The 'Drew' Gospel Manuscripts*, Unpublished Ph.D. thesis, Drew University, 1933 (see also 1275 and 1276) |
| | Clark, *USA*, pp. 38–9 |
| Plates | Clark 4 |
| | Sitterly (1914), XII |
| | Sitterly (1898), X |
| 668 | Complete collation by H. H. Severn, Unpublished M.A. thesis, University of Chicago, 1928 |
| | I. H. Hall, 'On a Cursive Ms. of the Greek Gospels', *Proceedings of the American Oriental Society* (New Haven, 1884), iii–iv and (1885), ccv–ccvi |
| | Clark, *USA*, pp. 216–17 |

| | |
|---|---|
| 669 | Brief description by J.R. Harris, in *Sunday School Times* (Philadelphia, 4 June 1887), 355 |
| | C.C. Edmunds and W.H.P. Hatch, 'The Gospel Mss. of the General Theological Seminary', HTS 4 (1918), 7, 50–68. Collation and 2 facsimiles (see also 2324) |
| | Clark, *USA*, pp. 83–5 |
| Plates | Clark 15 |
| 670 | Clark, *USA*, pp. 10–11 |
| 672 | Scrivener, *Adversaria* (as j) |
| Plates* | |
| 680 | Hoskier, *Text* 1, pp. 318–29 (for r) |
| 681 | |
| Plates* | |
| 684 | |
| Plates* | |
| 685 | D.O. Voss, 'K$^r$ Variants in Mk', in S. Lake, *Family Π and the Codex Alexandrinus*, *S & D* V (London, 1936), 155–8 |
| | Clark, *USA*, pp. 327–9 |
| 686 | |
| Plates | Pattie 1 |
| 688 | |
| Plates | Lake and Lake II, 82 |
| 690 | |
| Plates | Hatch LXXX |
| 691 | |
| Plates | Milligan, p. 161 |
| 693 | |
| Plates | Hatch LXXIX |
| 695 | |
| Plates | Hatch LXX |
| Plates* | |

| | |
|---|---|
| 696 | |
| Plates | Hatch LXI |
| 697 | |
| Plates* | |
| 698 | |
| Plates | Hatch LXXXI |
| 699 | Hoskier, *Text* 1, p.281 (for r) |
| | Scrivener, *Adversaria* (as δ) |
| Plates | Pattie 5 |
| Plates* | |
| 700 | Scrivener, *Adversaria* (as b) |
| | Description and collation, W.H. Simcox, *American Journal of Philology* V, 4 (Baltimore, 1884), 454–65 |
| | H.C. Hoskier, *A Full Account and Collation of the Greek Cursive Codex Evangelium 604* (London, 1890), and 2 facsimiles |
| Plates | Kenyon (1912), X |
| | Hatch XLIX |
| | Metzger, *Manuscripts*, 37 |
| | Pattie 2 |
| Plates* | |
| 703 | Edgar J. Goodspeed, 'The Bixby Gospels', *HLS* 4 (1915), 121–52 |
| | Clark, *USA*, pp.119–21 |
| Plates | Clark 26 |
| 706 | |
| Plates* | |
| 707 | |
| Plates* | |
| 708 | |
| Plates* | |
| 709 | |
| Plates | Wilson 27 |
| Plates* | |

| | |
|---|---|
| 712 | Treu, pp. 143–5 |
| Plates* | |
| 713 | Part collation of Matthew in J.R. Harris, 'Codex Ev 561: Codex Algerinae Peckover', *JBL* 4 (1886), 79–89 |
| | J.R. Harris, 'The First Tatian Reading in the Greek New Testament', *Ex* VIII, 23 (1922), 120–9 |
| 719 | |
| Plates | Bick 12; see also p. 27 |
| Plates* | |
| 725 | |
| Plates | Wittek 24 (also plate in C. Gaspar and F. Lyna, *Les Principaux Manuscrits à peintures de la Bib. royale de Belgique* I (Paris 1937)) |
| 726 | |
| Plates | Wittek 21 |
| 735 | |
| Plates* | |
| 740 | |
| Plates* | |
| 743 | Hoskier, *Text* 1, p. 423 (for r) (see also J. Schmid, *Th Q* 117 (1936), 151) |
| Plates* | |
| 745 | |
| Plates | Hatch XCIX |
| 747 | |
| Plates | Lake and Lake V, 189 |
| 757 | Hoskier, *Text* 1, pp. 513 f. (for r) |
| Plates* | |
| 758 | |
| Plates* | |
| 759 | |
| Plates* | |

| | |
|---|---|
| 760 | |
| Plates* | |
| 763 | |
| Plates* | |
| 771 | |
| Plates* | |
| 773 | E. von Dobschütz, 'The Notices prefixed to codex 773 of the Gospels', *HTR* 18 (1925), 280–4 |
| Plates* | |
| 774 | |
| Plates* | |
| 775 | |
| Plates* | |
| 776 | |
| Plates* | |
| 777 | |
| Plates* | |
| 778 | |
| Plates* | |
| 779 | |
| Plates* | |
| 780 | |
| Plates* | |
| 784 | |
| Plates* | |
| 785 | |
| Plates* | |
| 788 | |
| Plates | K. Lake and S. Lake, *Family 13 (The Ferrar Group) in Mark*, *S & D* XI (London/Philadelphia, 1941) |
| Plates* | |
| (788 | See fam. 13) |

| | |
|---|---|
| 791 | |
| Plates* | |
| 792 | Hoskier, *Text* 1, pp. 369–80 (for r) (and see J. Schmid, *ZNW* 59 (1968), 257f.) |
| 793 | |
| Plates* | |
| 794 | |
| Plates | Lake and Lake I, 40 |
| 796 | |
| Plates* | |
| 799 | |
| Plates* | |
| 808 | Hoskier, *Text* 1, pp. 509–13 (for r) |
| Plates* | |
| 809 | |
| Plates* | |
| 811 | |
| Plates* | |
| 820 | |
| Plates* | |
| 824 | Hoskier, *Text* 1, pp. 353 ff. (for r) |
| Plates* | |
| 825 | |
| Plates* | |
| 826 | J. Geerlings, 'Is Ms. 826 the archetype of Fam. 13a?', *JBL* 67 (1948), 357–63 |
| Plates* | |
| (826 | See fam. 13) |
| 827 | Collation by F. G. Carver, Unpublished Th. M. thesis, Princeton Theological Seminary, 1958 |
| 828 | |
| Plates | Plate II in J. Geerlings, *Family 13 in Matthew*, S & D XIX |
| Plates* | |

| | |
|---|---|
| (828 | See fam. 13) |
| 829 | |
| Plates* | |
| 832 | |
| Plates* | |
| 835 | |
| Plates* | |
| 839 | |
| Plates* | |
| 845 | |
| Plates | Turyn (1972), 142; description pp. 177 f. |
| Plates* | |
| 852 | |
| Plates | Turyn (1964), 73; description pp. 100 f. |
| 856 | |
| Plates* | |
| 863 | |
| Plates | Lake and Lake VIII, 318 |
| 866 | Hoskier, *Text* 1, p. 16 (for r) (see also 1918) |
| (872 | See fam. 1) |
| 876 | A. V. Valentine-Richards, *The Text of Acts and Codex 614 and its Allies* (Cambridge, 1936) (see also 614) |
| | Scrivener, *Adversaria* (as β) |
| | Henry A. Sanders, 'Manuscript No. 16 of the Michigan Collection', in *Philological Studies in Honor of Walter Miller, University of Missouri Studies* XI (Columbia, Missouri, 1936), pt 3, pp. 141–89 |
| | J. M. Creed, 'Two Collations of the Text of Acts in Codex 876: a Vindication of Mr. Valentine-Richards', *JTS* 38 (1937), 395–9 |
| | Clark, *USA*, pp. 282–4 |
| | In K. W. Clark, *Eight American Praxapostoloi* (see 223) |

| | |
|---|---|
| Plates | Clark 48 |
| 877 | |
| Plates | Barbour 25 |
| | Lake and Lake VIII, 330 |
| Plates* | |
| 886 | Hoskier, *Text* 1, p. 389 |
| 891 | Article in Russian by A. Michael in *Studia evangelica* V, *T & U* 103 (Berlin, 1968), pp. 198–201 |
| 892 | Collation by J. R. Harris, 'An Important MS of the New Testament', *JBL* 9 (1890), 31–59 |
| Plates | Metzger, *Manuscripts*, 29 |
| | Pattie 3 |
| | Hatch VI |
| | A & A 49 |
| 894 | J. N. Birdsall, 'Ms 894: A Collation and an Analysis', in *Biblical and Patristic Essays in Memory of Robert Pierce Casey*, ed. J. Neville Birdsall and Robert W. Thomson (Freiburg, 1963), pp. 20–4 |
| 895 | (= 2366) |
| Plates* | |
| 899 | |
| Plates* | |
| 900 | |
| Plates* | |
| 903 | Collated by J. Geerlings as appendix C to R. Champlin, *Family E and its Allies in Matthew*, *S & D* XXVIII (Salt Lake City, 1966), pp. 170–200 |
| | Treu, pp. 155–6 |
| Plates | Cereteli and Sobolewski II, 44 |
| 904 | Collated by J. Geerlings in appendix A to S. Kubo, *P$^{72}$ and the Codex Vaticanus*, *S & D* XXVII (Salt Lake City, 1965), pp. 161–96 |
| 905 | Clark, *USA*, pp. 69–71 |

| | |
|---|---|
| Plates | Clark 10 |
| Plates* | |
| 906 | Clark, *USA*, pp. 71–3 |
| Plates | Clark 11 |
| Plates* | |
| 910 | |
| Plates | New Pal Soc II, 118 |
| | Lake and Lake IX, 361 |
| Plates* | |
| 911 | Scrivener, *Exact Transcript*, pp. 72–3 (as g) |
| 919 | Hoskier, *Text* 1, p. 428 (for r) |
| 920 | Hoskier, *Text* 1, pp. 429–34 (for r) |
| 922 | Hoskier, *Text* 1, pp. 515f. (for r) |
| 924 | |
| Plates* | |
| 925 | Treu, pp. 130–1 |
| Plates* | |
| 927 | |
| Plates | Lake and Lake III, 116 |
| 928 | Treu, 148–50 |
| 929 | |
| Plates* | |
| 931 | |
| Plates* | |
| 932 | |
| Plates* | |
| 935 | Hoskier, *Text* 1, pp. 521ff. (for r) |
| | (See also Elliott: 322) |
| 938 | Treu, pp. 138–9 |
| 940 | |
| Plates* | |
| 941 | |
| Plates* | |

| | |
|---|---|
| 942 | Treu, pp. 119–20 |
| Plates* | |
| 946 | |
| Plates* | |
| 948 | |
| Plates* | |
| 951 | Treu, pp. 150–3 |
| 953 | |
| Plates* | |
| 957 | |
| Plates* | |
| 965 | |
| Plates* | |
| 969 | |
| Plates* | |
| 976 | |
| Plates* | |
| 978 | |
| Plates* | |
| 980 | |
| Plates | Lake and Lake III, 118 |
| (983 | See fam. 13) |
| 986 | Hoskier, *Text* 1, p. 535 (for r) |
| 990 | |
| Plates* | |
| 1006 | Hoskier, *Text* 1, pp. 688 ff. (for r) |
| (1009 | See 041 (fam. Π)) |
| 1015 | |
| Plates* | |
| 1016 | |
| Plates* | |
| 1017 | |
| Plates* | |

| | |
|---|---|
| 1022 | In K. W. Clark, *Eight American Praxapostoloi* (see 223) |
| | Clark, *USA*, pp. 365–7 |
| Plates | Clark 60 |
| | Metzger, *Manuscripts*, 44 |
| Plates* | |
| 1036 | |
| Plates* | |
| 1048 | |
| Plates* | |
| 1050 | |
| Plates* | |
| 1054 | |
| Plates | Kenyon–Adams, *Our Bible*, XXVIII |
| 1056[b] | Clark, *USA*, p. 181 |
| Plates* | |
| 1061 | |
| Plates* | |
| 1064 | |
| Plates* | |
| 1068 | |
| Plates* | |
| 1071 | Description and collation: K. Lake, 'Texts from Mount Athos', in *Studia biblica et ecclesiastica* V (Oxford, 1903), pp. 140–8 |
| | K. Lake, 'Codex Bezae and Codex 1071', *JTS* (1900), 441–54 |
| | B. H. Streeter, 'Codices 157, 1071 and the Caesarean Text', in Lake F/S, pp. 149–50 (see 157 (Streeter)) |
| | J. N. Birdsall, 'The Geographical and Cultural Origin of the Codex Bezae Cantabrigiensis', in *Studien zum Text und zur Ethik des Neuen Testaments*, ed. W. Schrage, *BZNW* 47 (Berlin/New York, 1986), pp. 102–14, esp. pp. 113 f. |

| Plates* | |
|---|---|
| 1072 | Hoskier, *Text* 1, p. 546 (for r) |
| 1074 | |
| Plates* | |
| 1075 | Hoskier, *Text* 1, pp. 546 ff. (for r) |
| (1079 | See 041) |
| 1079 | |
| Plates* | |
| 1080 | |
| Plates* | |
| 1083 | |
| Plates* | |
| 1085 | |
| Plates* | |
| 1089 | |
| Plates* | |
| 1091 | |
| Plates* | |
| 1094 | Hoskier, *Text* 1, pp. 600 ff. (for r) |
| 1099 | |
| Plates* | |
| 1101 | Treu, pp. 209–11 |
| 1107 | |
| Plates* | |
| 1108 | |
| Plates* | |
| 1113 | |
| Plates* | |
| 1117 | |
| Plates* | |
| 1120 | |
| Plates* | |
| 1149 | (See also Elliott: 322) |

| 1152 | Collation in Samuel A. Cartledge, *A Group of Gospel Manuscripts*, unpublished dissertation, University of Chicago, 1930 |
| | (See also 2394 and 2398a) |
| | Clark, *USA*, pp. 231–3 |
| Plates | Clark 42 |
| 1156 | |
| Plates* | |
| 1161 | |
| Plates* | |
| 1163 | |
| Plates | Lake and Lake I, 19 |
| Plates* | |
| 1164 | |
| Plates* | |
| 1165 | |
| Plates* | |
| 1166 | |
| Plates* | |
| 1168 | |
| Plates* | |
| 1169 | Collation (with 1173, 1204, and 1385) by S. New, 'A Patmos Family of Gospel Manuscripts', *HTR* XXV (1932), 85–92 |
| 1173 | Collation (with 1169, 1204, and 1385) by S. New, 'A Patmos Family of Gospel Manuscripts', *HTR* XXV (1932), 85–92 |
| 1175 | Collated by S. New in *Six Collations*, pp. 220–43 and plate VII |
| | W. L. Richards, 'Gregory 1175: Alexandrian or Byzantine in the Catholic Epistles?', AUSS 21 (1983), pp. 155–68 |
| Plates | A & A 50 |
| 1181 | |
| Plates* | |

| | |
|---|---|
| 1185 | E. Massaux, 'Collation du Codex 1185 (Sinai 148) du Nouveau Testament', *Le Muséon* 67 (Louvain, 1954), pp. 1–42 |
| | Collation by K. W. Ogden as appendix A to J. Geerlings, *Family E and its Allies in Luke*, *S & D* XXV (Salt Lake City, 1968) |
| Plates | Hatch, *Sinai*, 59 |
| 1186 | |
| Plates | Hatch, *Sinai*, 26 |
| Plates* | |
| 1187 | |
| Plates | Hatch, *Sinai*, 27 |
| 1188 | |
| Plates | Hatch, *Sinai*, 28 |
| 1189 | |
| Plates | Hatch, *Sinai*, 58 |
| Plates* | |
| 1190 | |
| Plates | Hatch, *Sinai*, 29 |
| 1191 | |
| Plates | Hatch, *Sinai*, 30 |
| 1192 | |
| Plates | Hatch, *Sinai*, 4 |
| 1193 | |
| Plates | Hatch, *Sinai*, 31 |
| 1194 | |
| Plates | Hatch, *Sinai*, 32 |
| 1195 | |
| Plates | Hatch, *Sinai*, 23 |
| 1196 | |
| Plates | Hatch, *Sinai*, 60 |
| 1197 | |
| Plates | Hatch, *Sinai*, 33 |

| | |
|---|---|
| 1198 | |
| Plates | Hatch, *Sinai*, 34 |
| 1199 | |
| Plates | Hatch, *Sinai*, 35 |
| 1200 | |
| Plates | Hatch, *Sinai*, 36 |
| Plates* | |
| (1200 | See 041 (fam. Π)) |
| 1201 | |
| Plates | Hatch, *Sinai*, 49 |
| 1202 | |
| Plates | Hatch, *Sinai*, 71 |
| 1203 | |
| Plates | Hatch, *Sinai*, 5 |
| 1204 | Collation (with 1385, 1169, and 1173) by S. New, 'A Patmos Family of Gospel Manuscripts', *HTR* XXV (1932), 85–92 |
| Plates | Hatch, *Sinai*, 37 |
| 1205 | |
| Plates | Hatch, *Sinai*, 38 |
| | Benešević II, 53 |
| Plates* | |
| 1206 | Treu, pp. 134–5 |
| Plates | Hatch, *Sinai*, 39 |
| | Benešević II, 68 |
| 1207 | |
| Plates | Hatch, *Sinai*, 6 |
| 1208 | |
| Plates | Hatch, *Sinai*, 51 |
| 1209 | Treu, pp. 122–4 |
| Plates | Hatch, *Sinai*, 3 |
| | Harlfinger *et al.*, 69–73 |
| Plates* | |

| | |
|---|---|
| 1210 | |
| Plates | Hatch, *Sinai*, 7 |
| 1211 | Tischendorf, *Anecdota*, p. 12 |
| | Collation in E. Muralt, *NT Gr* |
| | Treu, pp. 53−4 |
| Plates | Hatch, *Sinai*, 8 |
| 1212 | |
| Plates | Hatch, *Sinai*, 9 |
| 1213 | |
| Plates | Hatch, *Sinai*, 50 |
| 1214 | |
| Plates | Hatch, *Sinai*, 10 |
| 1215 | |
| Plates | Hatch, *Sinai*, 52 |
| 1216 | Collation by K. Lake (of Matt. 11) in *HTR* 21 (1928), 338 ff. |
| Plates | Hatch, *Sinai*, 11 |
| 1217 | |
| Plates | Hatch, *Sinai*, 25 |
| | Harlfinger *et al.* 153−7 |
| 1218 | |
| Plates | Hatch, *Sinai*, 12 |
| 1219 | |
| Plates | Hatch, *Sinai*, 13 |
| (1219 | See 041) |
| 1220 | Treu, 198−9 |
| Plates | Hatch, *Sinai*, 14 |
| 1221 | |
| Plates | Hatch, *Sinai*, 15 |
| 1222 | |
| Plates | Hatch, *Sinai*, 16 |
| 1223 | |
| Plates | Hatch, *Sinai*, 17 |

| | |
|---|---|
| (1223 | See 041 (fam. Π)) |
| 1224 | |
| Plates | Hatch, *Sinai*, 40 |
| 1225 | Treu, pp. 316–18 |
| Plates | Hatch, *Sinai*, 18 |
| 1226 | Treu, pp. 242–4 |
| Plates | Hatch, *Sinai*, 41 |
| 1227 | |
| Plates | Hatch, *Sinai*, 42 and 53 |
| 1228 | |
| Plates | Hatch, *Sinai*, 43 |
| 1229 | |
| Plates | Hatch, *Sinai*, 54 |
| 1230 | |
| Plates | Harlfinger *et al.* 108–11 |
| | Hatch, *Sinai*, 24 |
| 1231 | Tischendorf, *Notitia*, p. 64 |
| Plates | Hatch, *Sinai*, 19 |
| 1232 | |
| Plates | Hatch, *Sinai*, 72 |
| 1233 | |
| Plates | Hatch, *Sinai*, 73 |
| 1234 | |
| Plates | Hatch, *Sinai*, 61 |
| 1235 | |
| Plates | Hatch, *Sinai*, 62 |
| Plates* | |
| 1236 | |
| Plates | Hatch, *Sinai*, 63 |
| 1237 | |
| Plates | Hatch, *Sinai*, 74 |
| 1238 | Treu, pp. 153–4 |
| Plates | Hatch, *Sinai*, 48 |

Beneševič II, 66

| | |
|---|---|
| Plates* | |
| 1239 | |
| Plates | Hatch, *Sinai*, 78 |
| 1240 | |
| Plates | Hatch, *Sinai*, 44 |
| 1241 | Collated by K. Lake, *Six Collations*, pp. 3–25 |
| Plates | Hatch, *Sinai*, 45 |
| | A & A 51 |
| 1242 | |
| Plates | Hatch, *Sinai*, 55 |
| 1243 | Used as collating base in M.M. Carder, 'A Caesarean Text in the Catholic Epistles?', *NTS* 16 (1969–70), 252–76 |
| Plates | Hatch, *Sinai*, 56 |
| 1244 | |
| Plates | Hatch, *Sinai*, 20 |
| 1245 | |
| Plates | Hatch, *Sinai*, 46 |
| Plates* | |
| 1247 | |
| Plates | Hatch, *Sinai*, 75 |
| 1248 | Hoskier, *Text* 1, p. 746 (for r) |
| Plates | Hatch, *Sinai*, 64 |
| 1249 | |
| Plates | Hatch, *Sinai*, 47 |
| 1250 | |
| Plates | Hatch, *Sinai*, 76 |
| 1251 | |
| Plates | Hatch, *Sinai*, 65 |
| 1260 | |
| Plates* | |
| 1273 | D.M. Taylor, *The Oldest Manuscripts in New Zealand* (Wellington, 1955) |

| | |
|---|---|
| 1275 | Description, text, collation, and analysis by E. A. Overton, *The 'Drew' Gospel Manuscripts*, Unpublished Ph.D. thesis, Drew University, 1933 |
| | Clark, *USA*, pp. 40–1 |
| Plates | Sitterly (1898), XI |
| | Sitterly (1914), XIII |
| 1276 | Description, text, collation and analysis by E. A. Overton, *The 'Drew' Gospel Manuscripts*, unpublished Ph.D. thesis, Drew University, 1933 |
| | Clark, *USA*, pp. 41–2 |
| Plates | Sitterly (1898), XII |
| | Sitterly (1914), XIV |
| 1278 | H. C. Hoskier, *A Full Account of the Greek Cursive Codex Ev. 604* (London, 1890), appendix A, pp. 1–25 |
| Plates* | |
| (1278 | See fam. 1) |
| 1282 | Clark, *USA*, pp. 90–1 |
| Plates | Clark 17 |
| 1286 | |
| Plates* | |
| 1288 | |
| Plates* | |
| 1289 | Edgar J. Goodspeed, 'A Twelfth Century Gospel Manuscript', *Biblical World* X (1897), 277–80, and frontispiece |
| | Edgar J. Goodspeed, 'The Newberry Gospels', *AJT* III (1899), 116–37 (description and collation) |
| | Edgar J. Goodspeed, 'The Textual Value of the Newberry Gospels', *AJT* V (1901), 752–5 (text analysis) |
| | Edgar J. Goodspeed, *The Newberry Gospels* (Chicago, 1902) (description, collation, text, analysis, and 2 facsimiles) |

|  |  |
|---|---|
|  | Edgar J. Goodspeed, *Greek Gospel Texts in America* (Chicago, 1918), *Historical and Linguistic Studies*, Ser. I, vol. II, *Texts*, pp. 1−29, 174 (reprint of *The Newberry Gospels* (1902) |
|  | Clark, *USA*, pp. 145−7 |
| 1290 | E. J. Goodspeed, *The Haskell Gospels*, *HLS* 5 (1918), 155−68 and 1 plate |
|  | Collation in E. J. Goodspeed, 'The Haskell Gospels', *JBL* XXI (1902), 100−7 |
|  | Clark, *USA*, pp. 223−5 |
| 1295 |  |
| Plates | Hatch II |
| 1300 |  |
| Plates* |  |
| 1309 | Treu, pp. 314−16 |
| 1310 | Treu, pp. 320−2 |
| 1312 |  |
| Plates | Hatch, *Jer* 18 |
| 1313 | Treu, pp. 136−7 |
| Plates | Hatch, *Jer*, 11 |
| (1313 | See 041) |
| 1314 |  |
| Plates | Hatch, *Jer*, 12 |
| Plates* |  |
| 1315 |  |
| Plates | Hatch, *Jer*, 32 |
| Plates* |  |
| 1316 |  |
| Plates | Hatch, *Jer*, 33 |
| Plates* |  |
| 1317 |  |
| Plates | Hatch, *Jer*, 14 |
| Plates* |  |

| 1318 | |
| Plates | Hatch, *Jer*, 35 |
| 1319 | |
| Plates | Hatch, *Jer*, 36 |
| Plates* | |
| 1320 | |
| Plates | Hatch, *Jer*, 37 |
| 1321 | |
| Plates | Hatch, *Jer*, 15 |
| Plates* | |
| 1322 | |
| Plates | Hatch, *Jer*, 16 |
| Plates* | |
| 1323 | |
| Plates | Hatch, *Jer*, 38 |
| 1324 | |
| Plates | Hatch, *Jer*, 17 |
| Plates* | |
| 1325 | |
| Plates | Hatch, *Jer*, 65 |
| 1326 | |
| Plates | Hatch, *Jer*, 61 |
| 1327 | |
| Plates | Hatch, *Jer*, 66 |
| 1328 | Hoskier, *Text* 1, pp. 626 f. (for r) |
| Plates | Hatch, *Jer*, 46 |
| 1329 | Treu, pp. 131−2 |
| Plates | Hatch, *Jer*, 20 |
| 1330 | |
| Plates | Hatch, *Jer*, 48 |
| 1331 | |
| Plates | Hatch, *Jer*, 49 |

| | |
|---|---|
| 1332 | |
| Plates | Hatch, *Jer*, 6 |
| 1333 | |
| Plates | Hatch, *Jer*, 7 |
| 1334 | Treu, pp. 128–9 |
| Plates | Hatch, *Jer*, 21 |
| 1335 | |
| Plates | Hatch, *Jer*, 22 |
| 1336 | Treu, pp. 158–9 |
| Plates | Hatch, *Jer*, 52 |
| 1337 | |
| Plates | Hatch, *Jer*, 42 and 53 |
| 1338 | Treu, pp. 126–7 |
| Plates | Hatch, *Jer*, 23 |
| 1339 | |
| Plates | Hatch, *Jer*, 43 |
| 1340 | |
| Plates | Hatch, *Jer*, 8 |
| 1341 | |
| Plates | Hatch, *Jer*, 24 |
| 1342 | Mark collated by S. New in *Six Collations* and 1 plate |
| Plates | Hatch, *Jer*, 44 |
| 1343 | |
| Plates | Hatch, *Jer*, 9 |
| 1344 | |
| Plates | Hatch, *Jer*, 25 |
| 1345 | |
| Plates | Hatch, *Jer*, 55 |
| | Finegan, 24 |
| 1346 | Treu, pp. 117–19 |
| Plates | Plate IV in R. Chaplin, *Family* Π *in Matthew*, *S & D* XXIV (Salt Lake City, 1964) |

|  | Hatch, *Jer*, 5 |
| (1346 | See 041) |
| 1347 | |
| Plates | Hatch, *Jer*, 1 |
| 1348 | Treu, pp. 156–7 |
| Plates | Hatch, *Jer*, 58 |
| 1349 | |
| Plates | Hatch, *Jer*, 10 |
| 1350 | |
| Plates | Hatch, *Jer*, 28 and 59 |
| 1351 | |
| Plates | Hatch, *Jer*, 3 |
| 1352 | Hoskier, *Text* 1, pp. 634f. |
|  | Treu, pp. 141–3 |
| Plates | Hatch, *Jer*, 41 and 45 |
|  | Lake and Lake VI, 250 |
| 1353 | |
| Plates | Hatch, *Jer*, 30 |
| 1354 | |
| Plates | Hatch, *Jer*, 60 |
| 1355 | |
| Plates | Hatch, *Jer*, 31 |
| 1356 | Clark, *USA*, pp. 363–5 |
| Plates* | |
| 1358 | |
| Plates | Hatch, *Jer*, 19 |
| 1359 | |
| Plates | 1 plate in Colwell, *Four Gospels* |
| Plates* | |
| 1360 | Treu, pp. 345–7 |
|  | W. Brosset, *Mélanges asiatiques*, VI, pp. 269–86, from *Bulletin de l'acad imp des sciences de St. Petersbourg* 15 (St Petersburg, 1871), 385–97 |

| | |
|---|---|
| 1364 | |
| Plates | Hatch, *Jer*, 39 |
| Plates* | |
| 1365 | |
| Plates | Hatch, *Jer*, 40 |
| Plates* | |
| 1376 | Treu, pp. 360–1 |
| 1384 | Hoskier, *Text* 1, p. 628 (for r) |
| 1385 | Silva New, 'A Patmos Family of Gospel Manuscripts', *HTR* XXV (1932), 85–92 (cf. 1169) |
| Plates* | |
| 1386 | Collated in J. Geerlings, 'Codex 1386 and the Iota Phi R Group', in J. K. Elliott (ed.), *Studies in New Testament Language and Text*, Nov T Supplements XLIV (Leiden, 1976), pp. 209–34 |
| 1394 | |
| Plates* | |
| 1397[b] | Clark, *USA*, p. 60 |
| 1403 | Treu, pp. 62–3 |
| 1404 | |
| Plates* | |
| 1413 | |
| Plates* | |
| 1415 | |
| Plates* | |
| 1420 | Treu, pp. 227–8 |
| 1424 | Clark, *USA*, pp. 104–6 |
| Plates | Hatch VII |
| | Clark 24 |
| 1424 | According to B. H. Streeter, *The Four Gospels* (London, 1924), p. 84, fam. 1424 includes: M(021), 7, 27, 71, 115, 160, 179, 185, 267, 349, 517, 659, 692, 827, 945, 954, 990, 1010, 1082, 1188, 1194, 1207, 1273, 1293, 1391, 1402, 1606, 1675, 2191 (see also von Soden's I φ group) |

| 1432 | K. Lake, 'Texts from Mount Athos', in *Studia biblica et ecclesiastica* 5 (Oxford 1902), pp. 88–185 |
| 1435 | |
| Plates* | |
| 1438 | |
| Plates | Lake and Lake III, 115 |
| 1439 | |
| Plates* | |
| 1441 | |
| Plates* | |
| 1443 | |
| Plates | Lake and Lake III, 103 |
| Plates* | |
| 1444 | |
| Plates* | |
| 1446 | |
| Plates* | |
| 1452 | |
| Plates | Lake and Lake III, 92 |
| Plates* | |
| 1454 | |
| Plates* | |
| 1463 | |
| Plates* | |
| 1466 | |
| Plates | New Pal Soc I, 27 |
| Plates* | |
| 1473 | |
| Plates* | |
| 1474 | |
| Plates* | |
| 1476 | |
| Plates* | |

| | |
|---|---|
| 1482 | |
| Plates* | |
| 1483 | |
| Plates* | |
| 1485 | |
| Plates* | |
| 1486 | |
| Plates | Lake and Lake III, 111 |
| Plates* | |
| 1487 | |
| Plates* | |
| 1491 | |
| Plates* | |
| 1492 | |
| Plates* | |
| 1493 | |
| Plates* | |
| 1498[b] | K. Weitzmann, 'A Fourteenth Century Greek Gospel Book with Washdrawings', *Gazette des Beaux-Arts* 105 (Paris, 1963), 91–107 |
| | Clark, *USA*, p. 372 |
| Plates* | |
| 1500 | |
| Plates* | |
| Plates | Plate III in R. Champlin, *Family* Π *in Matthew*, *S & D* XXIV (Salt Lake City, 1964) |
| 1503 | Hoskier, *Text* 1, p. 629 |
| 1505 | E. C. Colwell, 'A Misdated New Testament Manuscript: Athos, Laura B. 26 (146)', in Lake F/S, pp. 183–8[1] |
| | *ANTF* 7 |

---

[1] Reprinted under the title 'Method Validating Byzantine Date Colphons: A Study of Athos Laura B. 26', in E. C. Colwell (ed.) *Studies in Methodology in the Textual Criticism of the New Testament*, *NTTS* 9 (Leiden, 1969)

| | |
|---|---|
| Plates | One plate in Colwell, *Four Gospels* |
| | Lake and Lake III, 110 |
| Plates* | |
| 1510 | Collation of gospels by Ernest Schneider in R. Nevius, *Divine Names in Luke*, *S & D* XXV (Salt Lake City, 1964) |
| 1518 | Scrivener, *Exact Transcript*, pp. 58−9 (as c) (cf. e) |
| | A. V. Valentine-Richards, *The Text of Acts in Codex 614 (Tisch. 137) and its Allies* (Cambridge, 1934) |
| 1522 | Scrivener, *Exact Transcript*, pp. 61−2 (as e) (cf. c) |
| 1528 | Clark, *USA*, pp. 66−8 |
| Plates | Clark 8 |
| | Vikan 65 |
| Plates* | |
| 1530 | Clark, *USA*, pp. 63−5 |
| Plates* | |
| 1531 | Clark, *USA*, pp. 355−7 |
| Plates | Clark 58 |
| Plates* | |
| 1538 | |
| Plates* | |
| 1542[b] | C. A. Phillips, 'The Caesarean Text, with Special Reference to the New Papyrus (sc. $P^{45}$) and Another Ally', *BBC* X (Leiden, 1932), 5−19 |
| 1551 | Hoskier, *Text* 1, p. 685 (for r) |
| 1555 | |
| Plates* | |
| 1556 | |
| Plates | Lake and Lake III, 107 |
| 1572 | |
| Plates* | |
| 1573 | |
| Plates* | |

| | |
|---|---|
| 1582 | K.W. Kim, 'Codices 1582, 1739 and Origen' *JBL* LXIX (1950), 167–75 (see 1739) |
| Plates | A & A 52 |
| | Lake and Lake III, 86 |
| Plates* | |
| 1583 | |
| Plates* | |
| 1586 | |
| Plates* | |
| 1597 | Hoskier, *Text* 1, pp. 676f. (for r) |
| 1603 | |
| Plates* | |
| 1611 | Hoskier, *Text* 1, pp. 356–65 (for r) |
| | *ANTF* 7 |
| Plates* | |
| 1615 | |
| Plates* | |
| 1617 | Hoskier, *Text* 1, pp. 710f. |
| 1626 | Hoskier, *Text* 1, pp. 712–17 (for r) |
| 1637 | Hoskier, *Text* 1, pp. 719f. (for r) |
| 1652 | Hoskier, *Text* 1, p. 720 |
| 1668 | Hoskier, *Text* 1, p. 724 (for r) |
| 1672 | Treu, pp. 343–4 |
| 1678 | Hoskier, *Text* 1, pp. 728–32 (for r) |
| 1686 | |
| Plates* | |
| 1688 | |
| Plates* | |
| 1689 | |
| Plates | New Pal Soc I, 78 |
| (1689 | See fam. 13) |
| Plates* | |
| 1693 | Clark, *USA*, pp. 196–7 |

| | |
|---|---|
| Plates | Clark 37 |
| Plates* | |
| 1696 | |
| Plates* | |
| 1698 | |
| Plates | Vikan 16 |
| 1699 | |
| Plates* | |
| 1701 | T.E. Conrad, *The Seymour Gospels* (Chicago, 1942) (a privately distributed Chicago University Ph.D. thesis) |
| 1702 | |
| Plates* | |
| 1704 | Hoskier, *Text* 1, pp. 686 ff. (for r) |
| (1709 | See fam. 13) |
| 1716 | |
| Plates* | |
| 1719 | Hoskier, *Text* 1, pp. 681 ff. |
| 1728 | Hoskier, *Text* 1, p. 684 |
| 1731 | |
| Plates* | |
| 1732 | Hoskier, *Text* 1, pp. 700–4 (for r) |
| Plates* | |
| 1733 | Hoskier, *Text* 1, p. 705 |
| 1734 | Hoskier, *Text* 1, pp. 706–9 (for r) |
| Plates | Lake and Lake III, 97 |
| 1739 | M.-J. Lagrange, *Critique textuelle* II, *La Critique rationelle* (Paris, 1935), pp. 470–1 |
| | E. von der Goltz, *Eine Textkritische Arbeit des zehnten bezw. sechsten Jahrhunderts*, *T & U* 2, 4 (Berlin, 1899) |
| | Otto Bauernfeind, *Der Römerbrieftext des Origens*, *T & U* 14, 3 (Berlin, 1923) |
| | Collated by K. Lake, J. de Zwaan and M. Enslin, *Six Collations*, pp. 141–219 |

K. and S. Lake, 'The Scribe Ephraim', *JBL* 62 (1943), 263–8

Aubrey Diller, 'Notes on Greek Codices of the Tenth Century', *Transcripts and Proceedings of the American Philological Association* LXXVII (Philadelphia, 1947), 184–8, esp. 186.

K. W. Kim, 'Codices 1582, 1739, and Origen', *JBL* 69 (1950), 167–75 (see 1582)

G. Zuntz, *The Texts of the Epistles: a Disquisition upon the Corpus Paulinum* (London, 1953), pp. 68–84; id., 'A Piece of Early Christian Rhetoric in the New Testament Manuscript 1739', *Opuscula selecta* ... (Manchester, 1972), pp. 284–90

J. Neville Birdsall, 'A Study of Ms. 1739 of the Pauline Epistles and its Relationship to Mss. 6. 424. 1908, and M', unpublished Ph.D. dissertation, (University of Nottingham, 1959); id., 'The Text and Scholia of the Codex von der Goltz and its Allies, and their Bearing upon the Texts of the Works of Origen, especially the Commentary on Romans', *Origeniana, premier colloque international des études origeniennes* (Monserrat, 1973) (= *Quaderni di Vetera Christianorum* 12, Bari, 1975), pp. 215–21

(See also Elliott: 322)

| | |
|---|---|
| Plates | A & A 53 |
| | Plates IV, V, and VI, *Six Collations* |
| | Metzger, *Manuscripts* 32 |
| Plates* | |
| 1740 | Hoskier, *Text* 1, p. 719 (for r) |
| 1745 | Hoskier, *Text* 1, p. 718 (for r) |
| 1746 | Hoskier, *Text* 1, pp. 718 f. |
| 1760 | Clark, *USA*, pp. 51–3 |
| 1771 | Hoskier, *Text* 1, pp. 710 f. |
| 1774 | Hoskier, *Text* 1, p. 720 |
| 1775 | Hoskier, *Text* 1, pp. 725 f. |

| | |
|---|---|
| 1776 | Hoskier, *Text* 1, p. 726 |
| 1777 | Hoskier, *Text* 1, p. 727 |
| 1778 | Hoskier, *Text* 1, pp. 664 ff. |
| 1780 ° | Norman A. Huffman, *The Text of Mark in the Duke New Testament*, unpublished M.A. thesis, Duke University, 1932 |
| | John L. Stokes II, *The Text of Acts in the Duke New Testament*, unpublished B.D. thesis, Duke University, 1932 |
| | Ferrell Pledger, *The Text of the Apocalyse in the Duke New Testament*, unpublished B.D. thesis, Duke University, 1937 |
| Plates | Plate in Duke University, *Library Notes* 51 and 52 (1985), 50 |
| | Clark 5 |
| Plates* | |
| (1780 | See fam. Π 041) |
| 1795 | |
| Plates | Vogels 12 |
| 1797 | Description and tables in E. Zomarides, *Studien zur Palaeographie und Papyruskunde* 2 (Leipzig, 1902); and in *id.*, *Die Durba'sche Evangelische-Handschrift* (Leipzig, 1904) |
| Plates* | |
| 1799 | In K. W. Clark, *Eight American Praxapostoloi* (see 223) |
| | Clark, *USA*, pp. 75–6 |
| Plates | Clark 13 |
| 1800 | Treu, pp. 74–5 |
| 1802 | (And 1803, 1804, 2439, *l* 796, *l* 1261, *l* 1262) |
| | In A. Deissmann, 'Handschriften aus Anatolien in Ankara und Izmit', *ZNW* 34 (1935), 262–84 |
| 1815 | |
| Plates* | |

| | |
|---|---|
| 1816 | Collation and description by J. Geerlings as appendix C in R. Champlin, *Family* Π *in Mark, S & D* XXIV (Salt Lake City, 1966), pp. 164–70 |
| Plates* | |
| 1821 | J. Sickenberger, *Römische Quartalschrift* 12 (1898), 58–62; and id., *Titus von Bostra, T & U* 21, 1 (Leipzig, 1901) |
| Plates* | |
| 1822 | |
| Plates* | |
| 1826 | Treu, pp. 212–13 |
| 1828 | Hoskier, *Text* 1, pp. 424–7 (for r) |
| Plates* | |
| 1829 | |
| Plates* | |
| 1831 | (See Elliott: 1891) |
| 1834 | Treu, pp. 104–5 |
| Plates | Cereteli and Sobolewski II, 41 |
| 1835 | |
| Plates* | |
| 1841 | Hoskier, *Text* 1, pp. 435 ff. (for r) |
| 1842 | |
| Plates | Pal Soc I, 131 |
| 1843 | |
| Plates* | |
| 1849 | Hoskier, *Text* 1, pp. 438 f. (for r) |
| Plates | Lake and Lake II, 48 |
| Plates* | |
| 1852 | Hoskier, *Text* 1, pp. 342–6 (for r) |
| 1854 | H. C. Hoskier, 'Manuscripts of the Apocalypse – Recent Investigations IV', reprint from *BJRL* 8 (1924), 1–40 and 2 plates |
| | Hoskier, *Text* 1, pp. 442–56 (for r) |
| 1858 | Treu, pp. 221–3 |

| | |
|---|---|
| 1859 | Hoskier, *Text* 1, pp. 697 ff. (for r) |
| 1862 | Hoskier, *Text* 1, pp. 459–62 (for r) |
| 1864 | Hoskier, *Text* 1, p. 736 (for r) |
| 1865 | Hoskier, *Text* 1, pp. 739 f. |
| 1867 | J. Geerlings, 'Codex 1867', in Clark F/S, *S & D* 29 (1967), pp. 51–8 |
| | Collation by J. Geerlings as appendix E of R. Nevius, *The Divine Names in the Gospels*, *S & D* XXX (Salt Lake City, 1967) |
| 1872 | (See also Elliott: 322) |
| 1874 | Hatch, *Sinai*, 1 |
| 1876 | Hoskier, *Text* 1, p. 463 (for r) |
| Plates 1877 | Hatch, *Sinai*, 77 |
| Plates 1878 | Hatch, *Sinai*, 67 |
| Plates 1879 | Hatch, *Sinai*, 21 |
| Plates 1880 | Hatch, *Sinai*, 22 |
| Plates Plates* 1881 | Hatch, *Sinai*, 2 |
| Plates | A & A 54 |
| | Hatch, *Sinai*, 68 |
| 1882 | H. C. Hoskier, *Collation of 604*, appendix D and plate (see 700) |
| 1885 | Omont, *Inventaire* IV (Paris, 1898), pp. 353 ff. |
| | Treu, pp. 145–8 |
| Plates* | |
| 1888 | Hoskier, *Text* 1, pp. 597 ff. (for r) |
| Plates | Hatch, *Jer*, 13 |
| Plates* | |

1889

Plates      Hatch, *Jer*, 34

1890

Plates      Hatch, *Jer*, 62

1891        Treu, pp. 140–1

W. J. Elliott, *An Examination of von Soden's I b 1 Group of Mss.* (Acts and Catholic Epistles only), unpublished Ph.D. thesis, University of Birmingham, 1974 (collations and plates of 1891, 522, 206, 429, 1831, 2, 296, 635)

Plates      Hatch, *Jer*, 4

1892

Plates      Hatch, *Jer*, 50

1893        Hoskier, *Text* 1, pp. 608 f. (for r)

Plates      Hatch, *Jer*, 26

1894        Hoskier, *Text* 1, pp. 610–15 (for r)

Hatch, *Jer*, 27

1895

Plates      Hatch, *Jer*, 2

1896

Plates      Hatch, *Jer*, 64

1897

Plates      Hatch, *Jer*, 29

Plates*

1898

Plates*

1900

Plates*

1901

Plates*

1903        Hoskier, *Text* 1, pp. 737 f.

Plates*

1905

Plates      Hatch XV

| | |
|---|---|
| 1906 | |
| Plates | Lake and Lake IV, 164 |
| | Omont, *Facs* (1891), 24 |
| Plates* | |
| 1908 | Complete collation in S. P. Tregelles, *The Greek New Testament* (London, 1861–72) |
| (1908 | See Birdsall: 1739) |
| 1910 | |
| Plates* | |
| 1913 | Matthaei (as s) |
| 1918 | Hoskier, *Text* 1, pp. 98–103, and 388 (for r) (see also 866) |
| 1922 | Karl Staab, *Die Pauluskatenen nach den handschriftlichen Quellen untersucht* (Rome, 1926), p. 110; id., *Pauluskommentare aus der griechischen Kirche aus Katenenhandschriften gesammelt und herausgegeben* (Münster/Westf., 1933), pp. 423–69 |
| Plates | Metzger, *Manuscripts*, 41 |
| Plates* | |
| 1926 | Matthaei (as i) |
| | Treu, pp. 291–2 |
| 1927 | Matthaei (as n) |
| | Treu, pp. 283–5 |
| 1928 | Matthaei (as q) |
| | Treu, pp. 302–3 |
| 1933 | |
| Plates | Omont, *Facs* (1891), 19 |
| | Lake and Lake IV, 157 |
| Plates* | |
| 1934 | Hoskier, *Text* 1, pp. 207 f. (for r) |
| Plates* | |
| 1944 | Collation by T. Kleberg, 'Eine aus Modena stammende Göteburger Handschrift der paulinischen Briefe', *Eranos* 52 (Uppsala, 1954), 278–81 |

| | |
|---|---|
| 1948 | Hoskier, *Text* 1, pp. 249–53 (for r) |
| 1952 | |
| Plates* | |
| 1954 | |
| Plates | One plate in Colwell, *Four Gospels* |
| 1955 | Scrivener, *Exact Transcript*, p. 62 (as e) |
| | Hoskier, *Text* 1, p. 293 (for r) |
| 1956 | |
| Plates | Pattie 16 |
| 1957 | Hoskier, *Text* 1, pp. 286 ff. |
| 1959 | |
| Plates | |
| 1960 | In K. W. Clark, *Eight American Praxapostoloi* (see 223) |
| | Clark, *USA*, pp. 35–6 |
| Plates | Clark 3 |
| | Sitterly (1898), VIII |
| | Sitterly (1914), X |
| 1962 | |
| Plates* | |
| 1992 | |
| Plates* | |
| 2000 | Hoskier, *Text* 1, pp. 356–65 (for r) |
| 2004 | Hoskier, *Text* 1, pp. 478 f. (for r) |
| 2005 | José M. Bover, 'Un notable códice biblico (2005 = α 1436) de la Biblioteca Escurialense', *Estudios biblicos* 4 (Madrid, 1934), 249–67 |
| 2012 | |
| Plates | Hatch, *Jer*, 51 |
| 2014 | Hoskier, *Text* 1, pp. 39–44 |
| 2015 | Hoskier, *Text* 1, p. 55 (see also Schmid, *Th Q* 117 (1936), 151) |
| | Scrivener, *Exact Transcript*, pp. 77–9 (as n) |

| | |
|---|---|
| 2016 | Scrivener, *Exact Transcript*, pp. 70−1 (as c) |
| | Hoskier, *Text* 1, p. 62 |
| 2017 | Matthaei (as t) |
| | Hoskier, *Text* 1, pp. 63−7 |
| 2018 | Hoskier, *Text* 1, pp. 74−8 |
| 2019 | H.C. Hoskier, 'Manuscripts of the Apocalypse − Recent Investigations V', reprint from *BJRL* vol. 8, pt 2 (1924) |
| | Hoskier, *Text* 1, pp. 79−84 |
| 2020 | Hoskier, *Text* 1, pp. 89−97 |
| 2021 | Hoskier, *Text* 1, pp. 108 f. (see also Schmid 2, pp. 27, 41) |
| 2022 | Hoskier, *Text* 1, pp. 115 f. |
| 2023 | Matthaei (as o) |
| | Treu, pp. 296−7 |
| | Hoskier, *Text* 1, pp. 142−5 |
| 2024 | Matthaei (as p) |
| | Treu, pp. 297−8 |
| | Hoskier, *Text* 1, pp. 146−9 |
| 2025 | Hoskier, *Text* 1, pp. 181−4 |
| 2026 | Hoskier, *Text* 1, pp. 185−92 |
| 2027 | Hoskier, *Text* 1, pp. 193−6 |
| 2028 | Hoskier, *Text* 1, pp. 197−204 (see also Schmid, *Th Q* 117 (1936), 152) |
| 2029 | Hoskier, *Text* 1, pp. 205 f. |
| 2030 | Treu, pp. 331−2 |
| | Hoskier, *Text* 1, pp. 209 ff. |
| Plates | Barbour 43 |
| 2031 | Hoskier, *Text* 1, pp. 212−17 |
| Plates* | |
| 2032 | Hoskier, *Text* 1, pp. 218−20 (for r) |
| 2033 | Hoskier, *Text* 1, pp. 229−31 |
| 2034 | Hoskier, *Text* 1, pp. 232−7 |

| | |
|---|---|
| 2035 | Hoskier, *Text* 1, pp. 246 ff. |
| 2036 | Hoskier, *Text* 1, pp. 254–60 |
| 2037 | Hoskier, *Text* 1, pp. 261–5 |
| 2038 | Hoskier, *Text* 1, pp. 266–70 |
| 2039 | Matthaei (as r) |
| | Hoskier, *Text* 1, pp. 282–5 |
| 2040 | Scrivener, *Exact Transcript*, pp. 72–3 (as g) |
| | Hoskier, *Text* 1, pp. 294–5 |
| (2040 | Se 911) |
| 2041 | Scrivener, *Exact Transcript*, pp. 73–4 (as h) |
| | Hoskier, *Text* 1, p. 296 |
| 2042 | Hoskier, *Text* 1, pp. 294 f.; see also *Text* 1, pp. 301–6 |
| 2043 | Tischendorf, *Notitia*, p. 60 |
| | Treu, pp. 73–4 |
| | See Schmid, passim |
| | Hoskier, *Text* 1, pp. 314–17 |
| 2044 | Hoskier, *Text* 1, pp. 464 ff. |
| 2045 | Hoskier, *Text* 1, pp. 466 f. |
| 2046 | Hoskier, *Text* 1, pp. 468–71 |
| 2047 | Hoskier, *Text* 1, pp. 470 f. |
| Plates* | |
| 2048 | Hoskier, *Text* 1, pp. 472 f. |
| 2049 | Hoskier, *Text* 1, pp. 474–7 |
| 2050 | H. C. Hoskier, 'Manuscripts of the Apocalypse – Recent Investigations III', reprint from *BJRL* vol. 7, pt 3 (1923) and 1 facsimile |
| | Hoskier, *Text* 1, pp. 480–8 |
| 2051 | Hoskier, *Text* 1, pp. 484–93 |
| 2052 | Hoskier, *Text* 1, p. 493 |
| 2053 | Hermann von Soden, 'Der Apokalypse Text in dem Kommentar-Codex Messina 99', *AJP* 35 (1914), 179–91 |
| | Hoskier, *Text* 1, pp. 494–505 |

| Plates | A & A 55 |
|---|---|
| 2054 | Hoskier, *Text* 1, p. 506 |
| 2055 | Hoskier, *Text* 1, pp. 507 f. |
| 2056 | Hoskier, *Text* 1, pp. 401–8 |
| 2057 | Hoskier, *Text* 1, pp. 409–16 |
| 2058 | Hoskier, *Text* 1, pp. 417–22 |
| 2059 | Hoskier, *Text* 1, pp. 517–20 |
| 2060 | Hoskier, *Text* 1, pp. 381–8 |
| Plates | Metzger, *Manuscripts*, 42 |
| Plates* | |
| 2061 | Hoskier, *Text* 1, pp. 524–7 |
| 2062 | Hoskier, *Text* 1, pp. 527 ff. |
| 2064 | Hoskier, *Text* 1, p. 536 |
| 2065 | Hoskier, *Text* 1, pp. 537–45 |
| 2066 | Hoskier, *Text* 1, p. 389 |
| 2067 | H. C. Hoskier, 'Manuscripts of the Apocalypse – Recent Investigations V', reprint from *BJRL* vol. 8, pt 2 (1924) |
| | Hoskier, *Text* 1, pp. 390–400 |
| 2068 | Hoskier, *Text* 1, p. 549 |
| 2069 | Hoskier, *Text* 1, p. 549 |
| 2070 | Hoskier, *Text* 1, pp. 550–5 |
| 2071 (and *l* 642) | Hoskier, *Text* 1, pp. 563–6 |
| Plates* | |
| 2073 | Hoskier, *Text* 1, pp. 567–71 |
| 2074 | Hoskier, *Text* 1, pp. 572–5 |
| 2075 | Hoskier, *Text* 1, p. 575 |
| 2076 | Hoskier, *Text* 1, pp. 576 ff. |
| 2077 | Hoskier, *Text* 1, p. 579 |
| 2078 | Hoskier, *Text* 1, p. 580 |
| 2079 | Hoskier, *Text* 1, pp. 581 f. |
| 2080 | H. C. Hoskier, 'Manuscripts of the Apocalypse – Recent Investigations V', reprint from *BJRL* vol. 8, pt 2 (1924) and 1 facsimile |

|  |  |
|---|---|
|  | Hoskier, *Text* 1, pp.583–91 (for r) |
| 2081 | Hoskier, *Text* 1, pp.592–5 |
| 2082 | Hoskier, *Text* 1, pp.366ff. |
| 2083 | Hoskier, *Text* 1, pp.603–8 |
| 2084 | Hoskier, *Text* 1, pp.616–20 |
| 2085 |  |
| Plates | Hatch, *Sinai*, 57 |
| 2086 |  |
| Plates | Hatch, *Sinai*, 66 |
| 2087 | Scrivener, *Adversaria* (as η) |
|  | Collation by H.C. Hoskier, in *A Full Account and Collation of 604*, appendix F (see also 700) |
|  | Hoskier, *Text* 1, pp.51f. (for r) |
| 2091 | Hoskier, *Text* 1, pp.621–5 |
| 2102 |  |
| Plates* |  |
| 2105 |  |
| Plates* |  |
| 2116 | Hoskier, *Text* 1, p.746 (not collated) |
| 2127 |  |
| Plates* |  |
| 2130 |  |
| Plates | Furlan III, 20 |
| 2131 | Treu, pp.335–8 |
| 2132 | Treu, pp.195–7 |
| 2133 | Treu, pp.309–11 |
| 2134 | Treu, pp.238–9 |
| Plates* |  |
| 2135 | Treu, pp.239–42 |
| Plates* |  |
| 2136 | Treu, pp.260–1 |
|  | Hoskier, *Text* 1, p.745 |
| 2137 | Treu, pp.261–2 |

| | |
|---|---|
| 2138 | Treu, pp. 328–31 |
| | *ANTF* 7 |
| | C.-B. Amphoux, 'La Parenté textuelle de Sy<sup>h</sup> et du groupe 2138 dans l'épître de Jacques', *Biblica* 62 (1981), 259–71 |
| | Hoskier, *Text* 1, pp. 743 ff. (for r) |
| Plates | Plate 4 in L. Vaganay, *Initiation à la Critique textuelle du Nouveau Testament*, 2nd edn. by C.-B. Amphoux (Paris, 1986) |
| | Cereteli and Sobolewski I, 20 |
| 2139 | Treu, pp. 76–7 |
| 2140 | Treu, pp. 77–9 |
| 2141 | Treu, pp. 79–81 |
| 2142 | Treu, pp. 81–2 |
| Plates* | |
| 2143 | Treu, pp. 82–4 |
| 2144 | Treu, pp. 90–2 |
| 2145 | Treu, pp. 92–5 |
| Plates | Cereteli and Sobolewski II, 26 |
| | Lake and Lake VI, 245 |
| (2145 | See 565 (Schmidtke)) |
| 2146 | Treu, pp. 95–7 |
| 2147 | Treu, pp. 97–101 |
| 2148 | Treu, pp. 105–7 |
| Plates | Cereteli and Sobolewski II, 49 |
| 2149 | Treu, pp. 48–50 |
| 2150 | Treu, pp. 117–19 |
| 2153 | Treu, pp. 122–4 |
| 2154 | Treu, pp. 126–7 |
| 2155 | Treu, pp. 128–9 |
| 2156 | Treu, pp. 130–1 |
| 2157 | Treu, pp. 131–2 |
| 2158 | Treu, pp. 134–5 |
| 2159 | Treu, pp. 209–11 |

| | |
|---|---|
| Plates | Cereteli and Sobolewski II, 38 |
| Plates* | |
| 2160 | Treu, p. 137 |
| Plates | Cereteli and Sobolewski II, 41 |
| 2161 | Treu, pp. 138–9 |
| Plates | Cereteli and Sobolewski II, 44 |
| 2162 | Treu, pp. 140–1 |
| 2163 | Treu, pp. 141–3 |
| 2164 | Treu, pp. 143–5 |
| 2165 | Treu, pp. 148–50 |
| 2166 | Treu, pp. 150–3 |
| 2167 | Treu, pp. 153–4 |
| Plates | Cereteli and Sobolewski II, 34 |
| 2168 | Treu, pp. 155–6 |
| Plates | Cereteli and Sobolewski II, 44 |
| 2169 | Treu, pp. 156–7 |
| 2170 | Treu, pp. 158–9 |
| Plates | Cereteli and Sobolewski II, 47 |
| 2172 | Treu, pp. 159–61 |
| 2173 | Treu, pp. 161–3 |
| 2174 | Treu, pp. 164–6 |
| 2175 | Treu, pp. 166–8 |
| 2176 | Treu, pp. 173–4 |
| 2177 | Treu, pp. 174–6 |
| 2178 | Treu, pp. 176–8 |
| 2179 | Treu, pp. 178–9 |
| 2180 | Treu, pp. 179–81 |
| 2181 | True, pp. 182–3 |
| Plates | Cereteli and Sobolewski II, 14 |
| 2182 | Treu, pp. 183–5 |
| 2183 | |
| Plates* | |
| 2186 | Hoskier, *Text* 1, pp. 678–81 (for r) |

| | |
|---|---|
| Plates | Vogels 17 |
| 2191 | |
| Plates* | |
| (2193 | See fam. 1) |
| 2194 | |
| Plates | Lake and Lake III, 114 |
| Plates* | |
| 2195 | |
| Plates* | |
| 2196 | Hoskier, *Text* 1, pp. 721 ff. |
| 2199 | Treu, pp. 225–7 |
| 2200 | Hoskier, *Text* 1, pp. 741 f. (for r) |
| 2222[a] | Clark, *USA*, pp. 251–5 |
| Plates | Clark 43 |
| 2228 | |
| Plates* | |
| 2229 | |
| Plates* | |
| 2248 | |
| Plates | Hatch, *Jer*, 47 |
| 2254 | Hoskier, *Text* 1, p. 691 |
| 2256 | Hoskier, *Text* 1, pp. 693–7 |
| 2258 | Hoskier, *Text* 1, p. 692 |
| 2263 | |
| Plates* | |
| 2267 | Treu, pp. 220–1 |
| 2269 | Treu, pp. 204–5 |
| 2270 | Treu, pp. 216–17 |
| 2272 | Treu, pp. 212–13 |
| 2273 | Treu, pp. 218–19 |
| 2274 | Treu, p. 216 |
| 2275 | Treu, pp. 205–6 |

2278

Plates      New Pal Soc I, 52

Plates*

2283

Plates*

2286      Hoskier, *Text* 1, pp. 733–5

2292

Plates      Bick, plate 14; description p. 28

Plates*

2297

Plates*

2298      (See also Elliott: 322)

Plates*

2302      Hoskier, *Text* 1, pp. 630–3

            Gregory, Textkritik III, pp. 1207–10

Plates      Hatch, *Jer*, 54

2303[a]

Plates      Hatch, *Jer*, 56

2303[b]

Plates      Hatch, *Jer*, 57

Plates*

2304      Clark, *USA*, pp. 91–3

Plates      Clark 18

2305      Hoskier, *Text* 1, pp. 559–62

2311      Clark, *USA*, pp. 184–5

Plates      One plate in B. W. Robinson, 'New Ms. Acquisitions for Chicago', *University of Chicago Magazine* XXI (1929), 240–3

2314

Plates*

2321      E. J. Goodspeed, Collation in 'The Toronto Gospels', *AJT* XV (1911), 268–71, 445–59; reprinted in E. J. Goodspeed, *Greek Gospel Texts in America, Historical and Linguistic Series* II (Chicago, 1918), texts 31–51

|  | Clark, *USA*, pp. 345–6 |
| Plates | Clark 52 |
| Plates* | |
| 2322 | D. O. Voss, 'K$^r$ Variants in Mk', in S. Lake, *Family Π and the Codex Alexandrinus*, *S & D* V (London, 1936), pp. 155–8 |
|  | Clark, *USA*, pp. 343–4 |
| 2323 | |
| Plates | Plate 30, Benaki Museum Catalogue: Δεκα Αἰωνες Ἑλληνικης Γραφης (Athens, 1977) |
| 2324 | E. C. Edmunds and W. H. P. Hatch, 'The Gospel Manuscripts of the General Theological Seminary', *HTS* 4 (1918), 7–33 and 3 facsimiles (669) |
|  | Clark, *USA*, pp. 80–1 |
| Plates | Clark 14 |
|  | Vogels 12 |
|  | Vikan 101 |
| Plates* | |
| 2325 | Clark, *USA*, p. 376 |
| 2326 | Clark, *USA*, pp. 49–50 |
| (2326 | See 2324 (Edmunds and Hatch)) |
| 2329 | H. C. Hoskier, 'Manuscripts of the Apocalypse – Recent Investigations I', reprint from *BJRL* 6 (1922), 1–20 (and facsimiles) |
|  | Hoskier, *Text* 1, pp. 637–52 |
|  | N. A. Beis, 'Die Kollation der Apokalypse Johannis mit dem Kodex 573 des Meteora Klosters', *ZNW* 13 (1912), 260–5 |
| Plates* | |
| 2344 | Collated by J. Schmid, 'Unbeachtete Apokalypse-Handschriften', *Th Q* 120 (1939), 154–87 |
|  | New collation in M. Davies, *The Text of the Pauline Epistles in Manuscript 2344 and its Relationship to the Text of other Known Manuscripts in Particular to 330, 436 and 462*, *S & D* XXXVIII (Salt Lake City, 1968) |

| | |
|---|---|
| Plates | A & A 56 |
| 2346 | E.C. Edmunds and W.H.P. Hatch, 'The Gospel Mss. of the General Theological Seminary', *HTS* IV, 7 (1918), 34–9 collation and 4 facsimiles |
| | Clark, *USA*, pp. 85–7 |
| | J. Geerlings, Discussion in 'Codices 2346 & 2491', appendix C of J. Geerlings, *Family* Π *in Luke*, *S & D* XXII (Salt Lake City, 1962), pp. 161–70 |
| Plates | Clark 16 |
| 2347 | Clark, *USA*, pp. 194–5 |
| Plates | Clark 36 |
| (2347 | = 1701) |
| 2349 | Hoskier, *Text* 1, pp. 440 f. |
| | Clark, *USA*, pp. 166–7 |
| Plates | Clark 32 |
| | Vogels 12 |
| (2349 | = 1795) |
| 2350 | Hoskier, *Text* 1, p. 529 |
| 2351 | H.C. Hoskier, 'Manuscripts of the Apocalypse – Recent Investigations II', reprint from *BJRL* vol. 7, pt 2 (1923), 1–12 |
| | Hoskier, *Text* 1, pp. 653–62 |
| 2352 | H.C. Hoskier, 'Manuscripts of the Apocalypse – Recent Investigations II', reprint from *BJRL* vol. 7, pt 2 (1923), 12–13 |
| | Hoskier, *Text* 1, pp. 663 f. |
| 2353 | Clark, *USA*, p. 275 |
| 2354 | Clark, *USA*, pp. 320–1 |
| 2355 | |
| Plates | Hatch, *Sinai*, 69 |
| 2356 | |
| Plates | Hatch, *Sinai*, 70 |
| 2357 | |
| Plates | Hatch, *Jer*, 63 |

| | |
|---|---|
| 2358 | John W. Bowman, *The Robertson Codex* (Allahabad, 1928). Reprinted from *The Indian Standard* 139, nos. 8 and 9 (August and September 1928) |
| | A. T. Robertson, 'A Newly Discovered Tetra-Euangelion', *RE* 25 (1928), 79–80 and see 'The Roberton Codex: Photographing a Greek Manuscript of the Gospels, Codex Robertsonianus – Minusc. 2358', *RE* 26 (1929), 171–96 |
| | John W. Bowman, *The Robertson Gospels*, Unpublished dissertation, Southern Baptist Theological Seminary, Louisville, Ky, 1930 |
| | Clark, *USA*, pp. 210–11 |
| 2363 | Clark, *USA*, p. 279 |
| 2364 | H. R. Willoughby, *Four Gospels of Karahissar* II (Chicago, 1936), pp. 372–438 |
| | Clark, *USA*, pp. 331–3 |
| 2365 | Clark, *USA*, pp. 330–1 |
| 2366 | Clark, *USA*, pp. 73–5 |
| Plates | Clark 12 |
| Plates* | |
| (2366 | = 895) |
| 2367 | Clark, *USA*, pp. 68–9 |
| Plates | Clark 9 |
| 2368 | Clark, *USA*, pp. 357–8 |
| Plates* | |
| 2369 | Clark, *USA*, pp. 350–1 |
| Plates | Clark 55 |
| Plates* | |
| 2370 | Clark, *USA*, pp. 348–50 |
| Plates | Clark 54 |
| Plates* | |
| 2371 | Clark, *USA*, pp. 359–60 |
| Plates | Clark 59 |
| 2372 | Clark, *USA*, pp. 358–9 |

| | |
|---|---|
| Plates* | |
| 2373 | Clark, *USA*, pp. 351–2 |
| Plates | Clark 56 |
| | Vikan 7 |
| Plates* | |
| 2374 | Clark, *USA*, pp. 353–5 |
| Plates | Clark 57 |
| Plates* | |
| 2375 | Clark, *USA*, pp. 361–2 |
| Plates* | |
| 2379 | J. Schmid, 'Zur Liste der NTlichen HSS.', *ZNW* 39 (1940), 241 |
| | D. Ionesco, *Mélanges offerts à M. Jorga* (Paris, 1933), pp. 877–94 |
| 2380 | Clark, *USA*, p. 89 |
| 2381 | Clark, *USA*, pp. 122–3 |
| Plates | Clark 27 |
| | Vikan 21 |
| Plates* | |
| 2382 | Clark, *USA*, pp. 149–50 |
| Plates* | |
| 2383 | Clark, *USA*, pp. 151–2 |
| 2384 | Clark, *USA*, p. 161 |
| Plates* | |
| 2385 | Clark, *USA*, p. 167 |
| 2386 | Clark, *USA*, pp. 168–9 |
| Plates | Clark 33 |
| Plates* | |
| 2388 | Clark, *USA*, pp. 99–100 |
| 2389 | Clark, *USA*, pp. 98–9 |
| Plates | Clark 21 |
| 2392 | Clark, *USA*, pp. 100–1 |
| 2393 | |
| Plates | Clark 22 |

| | |
|---|---|
| (2394 | See 1152 (Cartledge)) |
| 2394 | Clark, *USA*, pp. 235–8 |
| Plates* | |
| 2395 | J. Schmid, 'Zur Liste der NTlichen HSS.', *ZNW* 39 (1940), 241–2 |
| | (See also C. J. Papaioannu in *Theologia* 3 (Athens, 1925), 243–55) |
| 2396 | David O. Voss, *A Study of the Isaac, Hyacinthus, and Exoteicho Gospels*, Unpublished dissertation, University of Chicago, 1932 |
| | Clark, *USA*, pp. 241–3 |
| (2397 | See 2396 (Voss)) |
| 2397 | Clark, *USA*, pp. 245–7 |
| (2398 [a] | See 1152 (Cartledge)) |
| 2398 [a] | Clark, *USA*, pp. 238–41 |
| 2398 [b] | Collation in G. Abbott Smith, 'Two Uncharted Leaves of Gospel Parchment Minuscule Mss.', in *Canadian Society of Biblical Studies Bulletin* I (Montreal, 1935), 3–5 (see also 2415 [b]) |
| 2398 [b] | Clark, *USA*, pp. 32–3 |
| 2398 [c] | Clark, *USA*, p. 137 |
| (2399: | See 2396 (Voss)) |
| 2399 | D. O. Voss, 'K[r] Variants in Mark', in Silva Lake, *Family Π and the Codex Alexandrinus*, *S & D* V (London, 1936), pp. 155–8 |
| | Clark, *USA*, pp. 249–51 |
| 2400 | D. W. Riddle, 'The Rockefeller-McCormick Manuscript', *JBL* 48 (1929), 248–56 |
| | Ernest C. Colwell and Harold R. Willoughby, *The Four Gospels of Karahissar* (2 vols., Chicago, 1936), I, *History and Text* passim and plate I; II, *The Cycle of Text Illustrations*, passim and plates CXII, CXXIII |
| | Edgar J. Goodspeed, Donald W. Riddle, and Harold R. Willoughby, *The Rockefeller– McCormick New Testament* (3 vols., Chicago, |

1932), I, *Introduction and Color Facsimile*, II, *Text*, III,[2] *Miniatures* (125 plates)

(Reviews by B.S. Easton, 'The Rockefeller–McCormick New Testament', *ATR* XV, no.1 (1933), 46–50; C. Ward, *JR* XIV (1934), 211–13; A. Souter, 'Codex 2400', *ET* 45 (1933/34), 522–3; M.S. Enslin (II, *Text*) and Hugh S. Morrison (III, *Miniatures*), *JR* XIII (Chicago, 1933), 225–30; F.C. Burkitt (II, *Text*), *JTS* XXXIV (1933), 165–8; H.A. Sanders and Ernest T. De Wald, *Amer J Arch* XXXVII (1933), 521–2; *Times Literary Supplement* XXXII (December 1933), 894)

Clark, *USA*, pp.187–93

Plates     Harold R. Willoughby, 'Codex 2400 and its Miniatures', *Art Bulletin* XV, no.1 (New York, March 1933), 3–74, including 77 plates (3 in colour)

Clark 35

Plate in Colwell, *Four Gospels*

Vikan 80

Plates*

2401     K.W. Clark, *Codex 2401 – the Theophanes Praxapostolos*, Unpublished dissertation, University of Chicago, 1931

In K.W. Clark, *Eight American Praxapostoloi* (see 223)

2401[a]     (and *l* 1609)

Clark, *USA*, pp.256–9

Plates     Clark 44

Clark, *USA*, pp.137–8

2402     Clark, *USA*, pp.126–30

[2] Vol. III, p.359 contains a bibliography of articles on 2400 (see also H.R. Willoughby, *The Rockefeller–McCormick Manuscript and what became of it: A Bibliographical Record* (University of Chicago New Testament Department, 1943))

E. J. Goodspeed, E. C. Colwell and H. R. Willoughby, 'The Elizabeth Day McCormick Apocalypse', *JBL* 52 (1932), 81–107

H. R. Willoughby, *Byzantion* 14 (Brussels, 1939), 153–78

| | |
|---|---|
| Plates | Clark 28 |
| 2403 | J. Schmid, 'Zur Liste der NTlichen HSS.', *ZNW* 39 (1940), 241 |
| 2404 | Collation in A. E. Haefner, *The Scott Brown New Testament*, Unpublished thesis, University of Chicago, 1935 |
| | Clark, *USA*, pp. 227–9 |
| Plates | Clark 40 |
| 2405 | Clark, *USA*, pp. 233–5 |
| 2406 | Clark, *USA*, pp. 244–5 |
| | Otto F. Linn, 'The Tetragram, Thomas, and Larissa Gospels', Unpublished dissertation, University of Chicago, 1935 (and 2407, 2411) |
| (2407 | See 2406 (Linn)) |
| 2407 | Clark, *USA*, pp. 247–9 |
| 2408 | J. Schmid, 'Unbeachtete Apokalypse-Handschriften', *Th Q* 117 (1936), 151 f. |
| 2409 | Clark, *USA*, pp. 255–6 |
| 2410 | Emil K. Holzhäuser, 'The Georgius Gospels, the Text, Theodore of Hagios Petros and codex 89', Unpublished dissertation, University of Chicago, 1934 (2410 = 2266) |
| | Clark, *USA*, pp. 263–5 |
| Plates | Clark 45 |
| 2411 | Clark, *USA*, pp. 265–7 |
| (2411 | See 2406 (Linn)) |
| 2412 | In K. W. Clark, *Eight American Praxapostoloi* (see 223) |
| | Clark, *USA*, pp. 269–70 |
| Plates | Clark 46 |
| 2413 | Clark, *USA*, p. 56 |

| | |
|---|---|
| 2415 | Clark, *USA*, pp. 132–4 |
| 2415 [b] | G. Abbott-Smith, 'Two Uncharted Leaves of Gospel Parchment Minuscule Mss.', *Canadian Society of Biblical Studies Bulletin* I (Montreal, 1935), 3–5 (see also 2398 [b]) |
| | Clark, *USA*, p. 32 |
| Plates | Clark 29 |
| 2416 | Clark, *USA*, pp. 208–9 |
| | H. R. Willoughby, *The Four Gospels of Karahissar* II (Chicago, 1936), pp. 198 f., 342, 420 |
| 2417 | Clark, *USA*, pp. 25–6 |
| 2419 | J. Schmid, *Th Q* 117 (1936), 150–1 (see also Hoskier, *Text* 1, p. 423) |
| 2420 | Clark, *USA*, pp. 179–80 |
| Plates | Clark 34 |
| | Vikan 118 |
| 2421 | Clark, *USA*, pp. 57–8 |
| 2423 | In K. W. Clark, *Eight American Praxapostoloi* (see 223) |
| | Clark, *USA*, pp. 55–6 |
| Plates | Clark 6 |
| 2425 | Clark, *USA*, p. 272 |
| 2426 | Clark, *USA*, pp. 97–8 |
| Plates | Clark 20 |
| 2427 | E. C. Colwell, 'Some Unusual Abbreviations in ms. 2427', *Studia evangelica*, ed. K. Aland, F. L. Cross *et al.*, *T & U* 73 (Berlin, 1959), pp. 778–9 and 1 plate |
| | H. R. Willoughby, *The Rockefeller–McCormick NT* (Chicago, 1932), III, pp. 124–5 and plate XLII |
| | Clark, *USA*, p. 271 |
| | A & A 57 |
| 2436 | Hoskier, *Text* 1, pp. 672–6 |
| 2437 | B. M. Metzger, 'Un Manuscrito greco dos quatro evangelhos na Biblioteca Nacional do Rio de |

Janeiro', *Revista teológica* 2 (Rio de Janeiro, 1952–3), 5–10

2438 Clark, *USA*, p. 59

2439 A. Deissmann, 'Handschriften aus Anatolien in Ankara und Izmit', *ZNW* 34 (1935), 262–84 (and other MSS including *l* 796, *l* 1261, *l* 1262 and 1804)

2464 F. J. Leroy, 'Le Patmos St Jean 742', in *Zetesis* (Antwerp/Utrecht, 1973), 488–501 and plates

2464
Plates*
2466
Plates*
2467
Plates*

2472 E. Ioannides, Ὁ ἐν Κωνσταντινουπόλει Ἑλληνικὸς Φιλολογικὸς Σύλλογος 3 (1868), 107–14

2473 A. Papadopulos-Kerameus, Ἱεροσολυμίτικη Βιβλιοθήκη V (St Petersburg, 1915), 105–6

2474 D. M. Sarros, Ἐπετηρὶς Ἑταιρείας Βυζαντινῶν Σπουδῶν 8 (1931), 168–9

2475 K. W. Clark, *Bib Arch* 16 (1953), 38–9

2476 N. Camariano, *Biblioteca Academiei Romane. Catalogul manuscriselor greceşti* II (Bucharest, 1940), pp. 38 f.

2477
Plates H. R. Willoughby, *The Four Gospels of Karahissar* II (Chicago, 1936)

2478 C. Osieczkowska, *Studi bizantini e neoellenici* 6 (Rome, 1940) pp. 334–9 and plates

2479 A. Mancini, *Studi Italiani di filologia classica* 6 (Florence, 1898), pp. 460–1

2484
Plates Turyn, *GB*, 50; description p. 73
2487
Plates*

2491      Collation by J. Geerlings as appendix C to J. Geerlings, *Family* Π *in Luke, S & D* XXII (Salt Lake City, 1962)

2495      *ANTF* 7

2500      Treu, pp. 207−9

2502
Plates*

2505      A. Papadopulos-Kerameus, ''Ελληνικοὶ κώδικες ἐν τῇ βιβλιοθήκῃ τοῦ Πατριαρχείου Κωνσταντινουπόλεως', *Vizantijskij Vremennik* 17 (St Petersburg, 1911), 417

2506      G. A. Sotiriu, Κειμήλια τοῦ Οἰκουμενικοῦ Πατριαρχείου Πατριαρχικὸς ναὸς καὶ σκευοφυλάκιον (Athens, 1937), pp. 70−86; illustrations: 23 and 24, plates 46−59

2507      G. A. Sotiriu, Κειμήλια τοῦ Οἰκουμενικοῦ Πατριαρχείου Πατριαρχικὸς ναὸς καὶ σκευοφυλάκιον (Athens, 1937), pp. 92−3 and plate 63

2508
2509      A. Papadopulos-Kerameus, *Izvestija russakago archeologičeskago instituta v Konstantinopole* XIV, 2/3 (Sofia, 1909), pp. 113−14, 124, 126
2510

2529      Treu, pp. 318−20

2530      Treu, pp. 322−4

2533      J. N. Birdsall, 'A Report on the Textual Complexion of the Gospel of Mark in Ms. 2533', *Nov T* 11 (1969), 23−9

           R. G. Bailey, 'A Study of the Lukan Manuscript 2533 of the Gospels', *NTS* 23 (1976−77), 212−30

           *Catalogue 81: Precious mss., Historical Documents and Rare Books, the Majority from the renowned Collection of Sir Thomas Phillipps Bt., offered for sale by William H. Robinson* (London, 1950), item 15 and facsimile page

Plates*

| | |
|---|---|
| 2534 | Treu, pp. 206–7 |
| Plates | One plate in S. Lake, 'A Note on Greek Ciphers', in Lake F/S, pp. 365–7 |
| 2535 | Treu, pp. 213–15 |
| 2536 | Treu, pp. 219–20 |
| 2537 | Treu, pp. 229–30 |
| 2538 | Treu, pp. 185–6 |
| 2539 | Treu, pp. 186–8 |
| 2540 | Treu, p. 188 |
| 2541 | Treu, pp. 189–91 |
| 2542 | Treu, pp. 191–2 |
| 2543 | Treu, p. 194 |
| 2544 | Treu, pp. 199–202 |
| 2545 | Treu, pp. 303–5 |
| | K. Treu, *Fo und Fo* 38 (1964), 120 and 1 plate |
| 2546 | Treu, pp. 305–7 |
| 2547 | Treu, pp. 325–7 |
| 2548 | Treu, pp. 326–7 |
| 2549 | Treu, pp. 341–3 |
| 2550 | Treu, pp. 347–8 |
| 2551 | Treu, pp. 356–7 |
| 2552 | Treu, pp. 357–8 |
| 2553 | Treu, p. 358 |
| 2554 | |
| Plates* | |
| 2555 | |
| Plates* | |
| 2557 | |
| Plates | Plate 11 of Benaki Catalogue (see 2323) |
| 2561 | |
| Plates | Plate 6 of Benaki Catalogue (see 2323) |
| 2566 | |
| Plates | Plate 9 of Benaki Catalogue (see 2323) |

2576

Plates*

2592

Plates*

2595        Hoskier, *Text* 1, pp. 667–71 (for r)

2614        E. W. Saunders, 'The Textual Criticism of a
            Medieval Manuscript of the Four Gospels (Duke
            Ms. Gr 7)', Unpublished Ph.D. dissertation, Duke
            University, 1943

2626

Plates*

2628

Plates*

2633        Collation by J. Geerlings as appendix B to J. Geer-
            lings, *Family E and its Allies in Mk*, *S & D* XXXI
            (Salt Lake City, 1968)

2635

Plates*

2718

Plates*

2757

Plates       Plate in Duke University, *Library Notes*, 51 and 52
             (1985), 52

2787        Description and 2 plates in K. D. Ioannides, 'Τὰ ἐν
            Κύπρῳ σωζόμενα Χειρόγραφα Βυζαντινῆς
            Μουσιχῆς' Κυπριαχαὶ Σπουδαί 31 (1967),
            pp. 215–17, 249, 251 (see also A. Papageorghiou,
            *Masterpieces of the Byzantine Art of Cyprus*
            (Nicosia, 1965), pp. 33–4 and plate 42)

2790        Brief description and reproduction in K. D.
            Ioannides (see 2787)

# LECTIONARIES

*l* 1

Plates      Omont, *Facs* (1892), 21 [1]

Plates*

*l* 2

Plates      Omont, *Facs* (1892), 19 [4]

          Hatch, *Uncials*, LXXIII

Plates*

*l* 3

Plates      Hatch, *Uncials*, LXXII

Plates*

*l* 5

Plates      Hatch, *Uncials*, LXVI

Plates*

*l* 6

          H.J. de Jonge, 'Joseph Scaliger's Greek–Arabic Lectionary', *Quaerendo* 5 (Amsterdam, 1975), 143–72

          Anton Baumstark, 'Das Leydener griechisch–arabische Perikopenbuch für die Kar- und Osterwoche', *Oriens Christ* II, 4 (1915 (1914)), pp. 38–58

*l* 7

Plates      Omont, *Facs* (1891), 51

Plates*

*l* 13      B. de Montfaucon, *Bibliotheca Coisliniana* (Paris, 1715), pp. 84 ff.

Plates      Hatch, *Uncials*, LXXVI

          Omont, *Facs* (1892), 22

Plates*

*l* 14

Plates*

*l* 17

Plates      Omont *Facs* (1892), 18 [2]

Plates*

*l* 18

Plates*

*l* 20

Plates      Lake and Lake II, 57

Plates*

*l* 22

Plates*

*l* 30

Plates*

*l* 34

Plates      Silvestre

*l* 35

Plates*

*l* 36

Plates*

*l* 38      Matthaei (as v)

*l* 42

Plates*

*l* 46      (Purple MS: see also 080, 565, and 1143)

K. Weitzmann, 'Ein kaiserliches Lektionar einer byzantinischen Hofschule', in Festschrift K.M. Swoboda (Vienna/Wiesbaden, 1959), pp. 309–20

Plates*

*l* 47      Matthaei (as b)

Plates*

*l* 48      Matthaei (as c)

Plates      Lake and Lake VI, 227

Cereteli and Sobolewski I, 17

Plates*

*l* 49      Matthaei (as f)

*l* 50      Matthaei (as h)

Plates*

*l* 51      Matthaei (as t)

| | |
|---|---|
| *l* 52 | Matthaei (as ξ) |
| Plates* | |
| *l* 53 | Matthaei (as χ) |
| *l* 54 | Matthaei (as ψ) |
| *l* 55 | Matthaei (as ω) |
| *l* 56 | Matthaei (as 16) |
| *l* 57 | Matthaei (as 19) |
| *l* 59 | Matthaei (as b) |
| Plates | Hatch, *Mins*, XXXIII |
| | For facsimiles of other pages see C.F. Matthaei, *Novum Testamentum Graece et Latine* (Riga, 1782–8), V ad fin. |
| *l* 60 | |
| Plates | Lake and Lake III, 149 |
| | Omont, *Facs* (1891), 14 |
| Plates* | |
| *l* 62 | Matthaei (as e) |
| *l* 63 | |
| Plates | Hatch, *Uncials*, XLVII |
| | Omont, *Facs* (1892), 19[3] |
| Plates* | |
| *l* 64 | |
| Plates | Omont, *Facs* (1892), 19[1] |
| *l* 67 | |
| Plates* | |
| *l* 71 | |
| Plates | Lake and Lake IV, 173 |
| | Omont *Facs* (1891), 32 |
| *l* 72 | |
| Plates | Omont, *Facs* (1892), 20[3] |
| *l* 86 | |
| Plates | Omont, *Facs* (1891), 82 |
| Plates* | |

*l* 89

Plates*

*l* 90

Plates*

*l* 103

Plates*

*l* 107

Plates*

*l* 109

Plates*

*l* 111

Plates New Pal Soc II, 1, plate 4

Plates*

*l* 115

Plates*

*l* 116

Plates*

*l* 117

Plates*

*l* 120

Plates*

*l* 121

Plates*

*l* 122

Plates Lake and Lake VIII, 323

*l* 123 M. Bonicatti, 'L'evangelio vat gr 1522 ... Problemi di scrittura onciale liturgica', *Bibliofilia* 61 (Florence, 1959), 129–56

Plates*

*l* 125

Plates*

*l* 135

Plates*

*l* 136

Plates*

| | |
|---|---|
| *l* 139 | |
| Plates* | |
| *l* 143 | Ed. J. Leipoldt, *Aegyptische Urkunden aus der königlichen Museen zu Berlin* 1 (Berlin, 1904), pp. 147–8 |
| *l* 150 | Scrivener, *Exact Transcript*, pp. 47–50 (as H) |
| Plates | Pal Soc I, 26–7 |
| | Plate X in J. Scott Porter, *Principles of Textual Criticism* (London/Belfast, 1848) |
| | Barbour 3 |
| Plates* | |
| *l* 151 | |
| Plates* | |
| *l* 152 | |
| Plates | *Catalogue of Ancient Mss. in the British Museum* London, (1881), plate 17 |
| Plates* | |
| *l* 157 | |
| Plates | Turyn, *GB*, 5; description p. 16 |
| *l* 164 | |
| Plates | Lake and Lake V, 198 |
| *l* 170 | Clark, USA, pp. 313–14 |
| *l* 172 | Clark, *USA*, pp. 112–13 |
| | H. C. Hoskier, *A Full Account and Collation of the Greek Cursive Codex Evangelium 604* (London, 1896), appendix H (see also *l* 296, *l* 297, *l* 298) |
| *l* 173 | |
| Plates* | |
| *l* 175 | Clark, *USA*, pp. 142–4 |
| *l* 179 | |
| Plates* | |
| *l* 180 | G. C. Whipple, 'A Collation of the Lectionary of the Four Gospels, *l* 180, with the Textus Receptus', Unpublished Ph.D. thesis, Boston University, 1947 |
| | Clark, *USA*, pp. 3–4 |

| | |
|---|---|
| *l* 181 | Scrivener, *Exact Transcript*, pp. 50–2 (as P) |
| Plates | Pattie 17 |
| | Lake and Lake IX, 362 |
| Plates* | |
| *l* 182 | Scrivener, *Exact Transcript* p. 52 (as P²) |
| *l* 183 | Scrivener, *Full and Exact Collation*, p. lix (as x) |
| Plates | Hatch, *Uncials*, LXXIV |
| Plates* | |
| *l* 184 | Scrivener, *Full and Exact Collation*, p. lxi (as y) |
| Plates | Turyn, *GB*, 56; description p. 82 |
| Plates* | |
| *l* 185 | Matthaei (as z) |
| | Scrivener, *Exact Transcript*, pp. 52–5 (as z) and plate |
| *l* 188 | |
| Plates | Lake and Lake II, 68 |
| *l* 193 | |
| Plates | Turyn, *GB*, 67; description p. 99 |
| *l* 194 | |
| Plates | |
| *l* 195 | |
| Plates* | |
| *l* 197 | |
| Plates* | |
| *l* 203 | |
| Plates | Lake and Lake II, 59 |
| *l* 208 | |
| Plates | Lake and Lake V, 194 |
| Plates* | |
| *l* 216 | Scrivener, *Adversaria*, pp. lxvi f. (as u) |
| | Clark, *USA*, 317 |
| *l* 220 | Clark, *USA*, pp. 321–2 |
| *l* 223 | Scrivener, *Adversaria*, pp. lxvii-lxviii (as v) |

|  | Clark, *USA*, pp. 284–5 |
| *l* 224 | Clark, *USA*, pp. 308–9 |
| *l* 225 | Clark, *USA*, pp. 304–5 |
| *l* 226 | Clark, *USA*, pp. 302–3 |
| *l* 227 | Clark, *USA*, pp. 309–10 |
| *l* 228 | Scrivener, *Adversaria*, pp. lxxiif. (as zz) |
|  | Clark, *USA*, pp. 316–17 |
| *l* 233 |  |
| Plates | Pattie plate (on cover) |
| *l* 234 | C. Steenbuch, 'Evst. 234 (Scrivener: 227)', *JTS* XVI (1915), 416–19 |
| *l* 235 | C. Steenbuch, 'Evst. 235 (Scrivener 228)', *JTS* XVI (1915), 555–8 |
| *l* 236 | C. Steenbuch, 'Evst. 236 (Scrivener 229)', *JTS* XVII (1916), 180–3 |
| *l* 238 | H. I. B(ell), 'A Greek Evangelistarium from the Library of John Ruskin', *BMQ* 6 (1931/32), 87–8 |
| *l* 239 |  |
| Plates | Turyn, *GB*, 6; description p. 20 |
| *l* 242 |  |
| Plates | Cavallo 115 |
| *l* 243 |  |
| Plates* |  |
| *l* 244 |  |
| Plates* |  |
| *l* 245 |  |
| Plates* |  |
| *l* 246 |  |
| Plates* |  |
| *l* 247 |  |
| Plates* |  |
| *l* 248 |  |
| Plates* |  |
| *l* 250 |  |

| | |
|---|---|
| Plates* | |
| *l* 252 | |
| Plates* | |
| *l* 253 | S. Lake, 'A Note on Greek Ciphers', Lake F/S, pp. 365–7 and plate |
| Plates | Cereteli and Sobolewski II, 10 and 10a |
| Plates* | |
| *l* 257 | |
| Plates | Turyn *GB*, 47; description p. 69 |
| *l* 261 | |
| Plates* | |
| *l* 262 | |
| Plates* | |
| *l* 265 | |
| Plates* | |
| *l* 267 | |
| Plates* | |
| *l* 274 | |
| Plates* | |
| *l* 275 | |
| Plates* | |
| *l* 278 | |
| Plates* | |
| *l* 279 | |
| Plates* | |
| *l* 280 | |
| Plates* | |
| *l* 292 | |
| Plates* | |
| *l* 293 | |
| Plates* | |
| *l* 296 | Clark, *USA*, pp. 109–10 |
| | (See Hoskier *l* 172) |

| | |
|---|---|
| Plates | Clark 25 |
| | Hatch, *Uncials*, LVI |
| Plates* | |
| *l* 297 | (See Hoskier *l* 172) |
| | Clark, *USA*, pp. 110–12 |
| *l* 298 | (See Hoskier *l* 172) |
| | Clark, *USA*, pp. 113–15 |
| *l* 299 | (Written over 040) |
| | W. H. P. Hatch, 'A Redating of Two Important Uncial Manuscripts of the Gospels – Codex Zacynthius and Codex Cyprius', in Lake F/S, pp. 333–8 |
| *l* 300 | |
| Plates* | |
| *l* 301 | Clark, *USA*, pp. 36–8 |
| Plates | Sitterly (1898), IX |
| | Sitterly (1914), XI |
| *l* 302 | Clark, *USA*, pp. 82–3 |
| *l* 303 | B. M. Metzger, 'Studies in a Greek Gospel Lectionary (Greg. 303)', Unpublished Ph.D. dissertation, Princeton University, 1942 |
| | id., 'A Treasure in the Seminary Library', *Princeton Seminary Bulletin* XXXVI, no. 4 (March 1943), 14–19 |
| | On the earlier history of the manuscript, see Caspar René Gregory, *The Independent* (New York, 15 October 1888), 1343, and (24 January 1889), 111 |
| | Clark, *USA*, pp. 175–6 |
| Plates | Metzger, *Manuscripts*, p. 38 |
| Plates* | |
| *l* 313 | Clark, *USA*, pp. 310–11 |
| *l* 315 | R. Mathieson, 'An Important Greek ms Rediscovered and Reedited', *HTR* 75 (1984), 131–3 |
| *l* 330 | |
| Plates | Lake and Lake II, 84 |

Barbour 65

| | |
|---|---|
| *l* 331 | |
| Plates | Turyn, *GB*, 11; description p. 23 |
| *l* 334 | (See also 0133) |
| Plates* | |
| *l* 339 | |
| Plates* | |
| *l* 341 | |
| Plates* | |
| *l* 342 | |
| Plates* | |
| *l* 348 | |
| Plates* | |
| *l* 351 | |
| Plates* | |
| *l* 367 | |
| Plates | Omont, *Facs* (1892), 21[2] |
| *l* 368 | |
| Plates | Omont *Facs* (1892), 19[2] |
| *l* 372 | |
| Plates | Omont *Facs* (1891), 22 |
| | Lake and Lake IV, 163 |
| Plates* | |
| *l* 373 | |
| Plates | Omont *Facs* (1892), 18[1] |
| Plates* | |
| *l* 374 | |
| Plates | Lake and Lake IV, 175 |
| | Omont *Facs* (1891), 34 |
| Plates* | |
| *l* 375 | |
| Plates | Lake and Lake V, 203 |
| Plates* | |

*l* 381      M.R. James, *A Descriptive Catalogue of the second series of fifty mss (no. 51–100) in the collection of Henry Yates Thompson* (Cambridge, 1902), pp. 353–7

M.W. Redus, *The Text of the Major Festivals of the Menologion in the Greek Gospel Lectionary, Studies in the Lectionary Text* II, 2 (Chicago, 1936)

Harold R. Willoughby, *The Four Gospels of Karahissar* (Chicago, 1936), II, passim and plate CXXIV (19v)

K. Weitzmann, 'The Constantinopolitan Lectionary', in *Studies in Art and Literature*, Festschrift for Belle da Costa Greene (Princeton, 1954), pp. 358 ff.

Clark, *USA*, pp. 155–8

Plates      Clark 30

Plates*

*l* 383

Plates*

*l* 384

Plates*

*l* 385

Plates*

*l* 386

Plates*

*l* 387

Plates*

*l* 390

Plates*

*l* 392

Plates*

*l* 393

Plates*

*l* 394

Plates*

| | |
|---|---|
| *l* 401 | |
| Plates | Lake and Lake X, 375 |
| Plates* | |
| *l* 402 | |
| Plates | Lake and Lake I, 38 |
| Plates* | |
| *l* 404 | |
| Plates* | |
| *l* 408 | |
| Plates* | |
| *l* 409 | |
| Plates* | |
| *l* 412 | |
| Plates* | |
| *l* 414 | |
| Plates* | |
| *l* 416 | |
| Plates* | |
| *l* 425 | |
| Plates* | |
| *l* 428 | |
| Plates* | |
| *l* 429 | |
| Plates* | |
| *l* 430 | |
| Plates* | |
| *l* 432 | |
| Plates* | |
| *l* 433 | |
| Plates* | |
| *l* 434 | |
| Plates* | |

*l* 437

Plates*

*l* 441

Plates*

*l* 442

Plates*

*l* 444

Plates*

*l* 445

Plates*

*l* 447

Plates*

*l* 448

Plates*

*l* 449

Plates*

*l* 451     Description by P. Easterling, *Transactions of the Cambridge Bibliographical Society* 4 (Cambridge, 1966), p. 191

*l* 464

Plates*

*l* 465

Plates*

*l* 476     Scrivener, *Adversaria* (as x)

Clark, *USA*, p. 318

*l* 484

Plates*

*l* 495

Plates*

*l* 513

Plates*

*l* 516

Plates*

*l* 520

Plates      Lake and Lake IX, 355

Plates*

*l* 529

Plates*

*l* 531

Plates*

*l* 532

Plates*

*l* 534

Plates*

*l* 541

Plates*

*l* 542

Plates      Cavallo 114

Plates*

*l* 543

Plates*

*l* 547      J. Geerlings, *The Ferrar Lectionary (Cod Vat gr 1217, Greg 547)*, S & D XVIII (Salt Lake City, 1959) and 1 plate

              (See also 250: Birdsall)

Plates*

*l* 550

Plates*

*l* 554

Plates*

*l* 562

Plates      Metzger, *Manuscripts*, 33

              Lefort and Cochez 60

              Barbour 39

              Metzger, *Text*, 10

              Lake and Lake VII, 266

              Cavalieri and Lietzmann 17

Pal Soc II, 93

Plates 33–5, 43 in G. Vitelli and C. Paoli,
*Collezione Fiorentina di facsimili paleographici
Greci and Latini* (Florence, 1884–97)

Plates*

*l* 563

Plates*

*l* 570

Plates*

*l* 573

Plates*

*l* 586    J.N. Birdsall, 'Two Lectionaries in Birmingham',
*JTS* XXXV (1984), 448–54

*l* 595

Plates    Graux and Martin 38

Plates*

*l* 598

Plates*

*l* 613

Plates*

*l* 628

Plates*

*l* 632

Plates*

*l* 635

Plates*

*l* 636

Plates*

*l* 637

Plates*

*l* 639

Plates*

*l* 642    (See also 2071)

Plates*

*l* 643
Plates*
*l* 644
Plates*
*l* 650
Plates*
*l* 662
Plates*
*l* 672
Plates*
*l* 690
Plates*
*l* 693
Plates*
*l* 696
Plates*
*l* 698
Plates*
*l* 704
Plates*
*l* 708
Plates*
*l* 710
Plates         Lake and Lake VI, 252
                Cereteli and Sobolewski II, 30
*l* 711
Plates         Beneševic II, 79
Plates*
*l* 717
Plates*
*l* 718
Plates

*l* 719

Plates*

*l* 720

Plates

*l* 722      Photographic reproduction in J. Thibaut, *Byz Z* 8 (Leipzig, 1899), plate 1

Plates*

*l* 725

Plates*

*l* 748

Plates*

*l* 754

Plates*

*l* 757

Plates*

*l* 767      Collation: appendix A to J. Geerlings, *Family E and its Allies in Mark*, *S & D* XXXI (Salt Lake City, 1968), pp. 70–87

*l* 783

Plates*

(*l* 796      See 1802 (Deissmann))

*l* 798

Plates*

*l* 800

Plates*

*l* 805

Plates*

*l* 806

Plates*

*l* 807

Plates*

*l* 808

Plates*

| | |
|---|---|
| *l* 809 | Sakae Kubo, 'The Catholic Epistles in the Greek Lectionary: a Preliminary Investigation', *AUSS* I (1963), 65–70 |
| | Ronald E. Cocroft, *A Study of the Pauline Lessons in the Matthean Section of the Greek Lectionary*, *S & D* XXII (Salt Lake City, 1968) |
| | Klaus Junack, 'Zu den griechischen Lektionaren und ihrer Überlieferung der Katholischen Briefe', in *Die alten Übersetzungen des Neuen Testaments, die Kirchenväterzitate und Lektionare*, ed. K. Aland *ANTF* 5 (Berlin/New York, 1972), pp. 498–591 |
| Plates | Metzger, *Manuscripts*, 39 |
| *l* 812 | |
| Plates* | |
| *l* 813 | |
| Plates | Lake and Lake I, 22 |
| Plates* | |
| *l* 815 | |
| Plates* | |
| *l* 819 | |
| Plates* | |
| *l* 820 | |
| Plates* | |
| *l* 822 | |
| Plates* | |
| *l* 823 | |
| Plates* | |
| *l* 825 | |
| Plates* | |
| *l* 827 | |
| Plates* | |
| *l* 835 | |
| Plates | Lake and Lake III, 108 |
| Plates* | |

*l* 844

Plates       Plates 1–4, Harlfinger *et al.*

            Plate Jᵃ in L. Politis, 'Nouveaux manuscrits grecs
            découverts au Mont Sinai', *Scriptorium* 34
            (Brussels, 1980), 5–17

*l* 845

Plates*

*l* 846

*Plates**

*l* 847

Plates       Beneševič II, 41

Plates       Plate 59, Harlfinger *et al.*

            Beneševič II, 41

Plates*

*l* 850

Plates*

*l* 851

Plates*

*l* 852       K. Junack, 'Zu einem neuentdeckten
            Unzialfragment des Matthäus-Evangeliums', *NTS*
            16 (1969–70), 284–8

            I. A. Sparks, 'A New Uncial Fragment of St.
            Matthew', *JBL* 88 (1969), 201–2 (i.e. 087: q.v.)

*l* 854

Plates       Plates 123–7, Harlfinger *et al.*

Plates*

*l* 855

Plates       Plates 132–5, Harlfinger *et al.*

Plates*

*l* 857

Plates       Plates 36–40, Harlfinger *et al.*

            Beneševič II, 46

Plates*

| | |
|---|---|
| *l* 862 | |
| Plates* | |
| *l* 865 | |
| Plates | Plates 32–5, Harlfinger *et al.* |
| | Benešević II, 45 |
| Plates* | |
| *l* 866 | |
| Plates | Plates 128–31, Harlfinger *et al.* |
| *l* 868 | |
| Plates | Benešević II, 55 |
| | Plates 95–8, Harlfinger *et al.* |
| Plates* | |
| *l* 881 | |
| Plates* | |
| *l* 891 | |
| Plates | Plates 91–4, Harlfinger *et al.* |
| *l* 901 | |
| Plates | Lake and Lake VI, 257 |
| | Benešević II, 59 |
| Plates* | |
| *l* 907 | |
| Plates* | |
| *l* 910 | |
| Plates | Lake and Lake VI, 257 |
| *l* 914 | |
| Plates | Benešević II, 76 |
| Plates* | |
| *l* 916 | |
| Plates | Benešević II, 57 |
| Plates* | |
| *l* 924 | |
| Plates* | |
| *l* 929 | Clark, *USA*, pp. 221–2 |
| *l* 951 | Clark, *USA*, pp. 43–4 |

| | |
|---|---|
| Plates | Sitterly (1914), XV |
| | Sitterly (1898), XIII |
| *l* 952 | Clark, *USA*, pp. 44–6 |
| Plates | Sitterly (1898), XIV |
| | Sitterly (1914), XVI |
| *l* 953 | Clark, *USA*, pp. 46–7 |
| *l* 954 | Clark, *USA*, pp. 47–8 |
| Plates | Sitterly (1898), XV |
| | Sitterly (1914), III, XVII |
| *l* 955 | Clark, *USA*, pp. 15–16 |
| | S.P. Tate, *The Synaxarion of the Greek Gospel Lectionary: A Study of Gregory Nr l 955*, Unpublished thesis, Brown University |
| *l* 956 | Clark, *USA*, pp. 141–2 |
| *l* 961 | |
| *l* 962 | |
| *l* 963 | Published by E. Amélineau, *Notice*, pp. 363–424 |
| *l* 964 | |
| *l* 965 | |
| *l* 974 | |
| Plates | A & A 59 |
| *l* 990 | |
| Plates* | |
| *l* 1000 | |
| Plates | Lake and Lake I, 5 |
| *l* 1003a | |
| Plates* | |
| *l* 1003b | |
| Plates | Lake and Lake I, 4 |
| *l* 1005 | |
| Plates* | |
| *l* 1008 | |
| Plates* | |

*l* 1013

Plates        Lake and Lake I, 14

Plates*

*l* 1019

Plates*

*l* 1027        H. J. de Jonge, 'Een nieuwe Tekstgetuige van het
               Griekse Nieuwe Testament in Nederland',
               *Nederlands Theologisch Tijdschrift* 32
               (Wangeningen, 1978), 305–9; id., 'A New Witness
               of the Greek New Testament in Holland',
               *Quarendo* 9 (Amsterdam, 1979), 343–9

*l* 1029        Clark, *USA*, pp. 367–71

               H. R. Willoughby, *The Four Gospels of Karahissar*
               II (Chicago, 1936), p. 74

Plates*

*l* 1033

Plates        Lake and Lake I, 11

               Barbour 35

*l* 1043        C. Wessely, *Stud zur Pal und Pap* 12, pp. 231–40
               (see also K. Gamber, 'Fragmente eines griechischen
               Perikopenbuches des 5 Jahrhunderts aus Aegypten',
               *Oriens Christ* 44 (1960), 75–81

*l* 1075

Plates        Lake and Lake III, 99

*l* 1076

Plates*

*l* 1077

Plates*

*l* 1086

Plates*

*l* 1091

Plates*

*l* 1100

Plates*

*l* 1101
Plates*
*l* 1103
Plates*
*l* 1109
Plates*
*l* 1114
Plates*
*l* 1127
Plates          Lake and Lake III, 119
*l* 1141
Plates          Lake and Lake III, 113
*l* 1145
Plates*
*l* 1149
Plates*
*l* 1150
Plates*
*l* 1183
Plates          Lake and Lake III, 121
*l* 1183
Plates*
*l* 1215          D. Serruys, *Rev des bibliothèques* 13 (Paris, 1903), 58
*l* 1222
Plates*
*l* 1224
Plates*
*l* 1227
Plates*
*l* 1228
Plates*
*l* 1229
Plates*

*l* 1230

Plates*

*l* 1231     E.C. Colwell and D.W. Riddle (eds.), *Prolegomena to the Study of the Lectionary Text of the Gospels, Studies in the Lectionary Text* I (Chicago, 1933) (includes the collation of *l* 1599, *l* 1627 and *l* 1642)

    Allen P. Wikgren, *The Scheide Gospel Lectionary*, Unpublished M.A. thesis, University of Chicago, 1929

    M.W. Redus, *The Text of the Major Festivals of the Menologion in the Greek Gospel Lectionary, Studies in the Lectionary Text* II, 2 (Chicago, 1936)

    Clark, *USA*, pp. 197–200

Plates     Vikan 3

    Clark 38

(*l* 1261, *l* 1262: see 1802 (Deissmann))

*l* 1265

Plates     Turyn (1972) 8; description pp. 18f.

*l* 1274     J. Thibaut, *Byz Z* 8 (Leipzig, 1899), 124 and plate 2

Plates*

*l* 1276     C. Taylor, *Hebrew Greek Cairo Genizah Palimpsests from the Taylor-Schechter Collection* (Cambridge, 1900), pp. 82–92 and plate

*l* 1286

Plates     Lake and Lake X, 387

Plates*

*l* 1296

Plates*

*l* 1304

Plates*

*l* 1311     Matthaei (as tz)

*l* 1318     Clark, *USA*, pp. 27–8, 173

*l* 1320

Plates*

*l* 1345

Plates*

*l* 1346    Ed. Bianchini (1740)

*l* 1347    Ed. Bianchini (1740)

*l* 1348

Plates    Cavallo 112

Plates*

*l* 1351    Description: Montfaucon, *Palaeographia Graeca* (Paris, 1708), pp. 235–47

*l* 1353    NT portions published by P. J. Balestri, *Fragmenta Musei Borgiani* (Rome 1901), pp. lii–lviii, 40–1, 91, 123, 308 (and p. 316: plate)

*l* 1354    Description and collation of additional leaf in A. Passoni dell'Acqua, 'Frammenti inediti del Vangelo secondo Matteo', in *Aegyptus* 60 (1980), 96–119, with plates

*l* 1355

Plates    Wilson 6

*l* 1371

Plates*

*l* 1372    Facsimile and transcription of 1 page in E. C. Mitchell, *Critical Handbook of the Greek New Testament*, 2nd edn (New York, 1896), p. 232

Clark, *USA*, pp. 218–19

*l* 1373    Clark, *USA*, pp. 219–20

*l* 1374

Plates    Lake and Lake I, 41

Plates*

*l* 1386

Plates*

*l* 1391

Plates    Lake and Lake VI, 239

Cereteli and Sobolewski II, 11

*l* 1392

Plates    Lefort and Cochez 55

| | |
|---|---|
| | Cereteli and Sobolewski II, 4 |
| *l* 1395 | |
| Plates* | |
| *l* 1399 | |
| Plates | Cereteli and Sobolewski II, 9 |
| *l* 1401 | |
| Plates | Cereteli and Sobolewski II, 12 |
| *l* 1402 | Treu, pp. 124–6 |
| *l* 1405 | |
| Plates | Cereteli and Sobolewski II, 24 |
| *l* 1406 | |
| Plates | Cereteli and Sobolewski II, 31 |
| *l* 1414 | |
| Plates | Lake and Lake VI, 247 |
| *l* 1417 | |
| Plates | Beneševic II, 48 |
| Plates* | |
| *l* 1426 | |
| Plates | Lake and Lake VI, 246 |
| *l* 1443 | Collation by A. Kuo, Unpublished Th.M. thesis, Princeton Theological Seminary, 1962 |
| Plates | Lake and Lake VI, 257 |
| | Beneševic II, 51 |
| | Harlfinger, *et al.*, 60–3 |
| Plates* | |
| *l* 1468[a] | |
| Plates* | |
| *l* 1491 | |
| Plates | Lake and Lake II, 67 |
| | Barbour 62 |
| *l* 1498 | |
| Plates* | |

*l* 1523

Plates*

*l* 1525

Plates*

*l* 1527

Plates*

*l* 1530

Plates*

*l* 1533

Plates*

*l* 1536      Clark, *USA*, pp. 93–4

Plates      Clark 19

*l* 1539

Plates*

*l* 1540

Plates*

*l* 1546      Clark, *USA*, p. 34

*l* 1547      Clark, *USA*, pp. 30–1

*l* 1552

Plates      Lake and Lake VI, 236

*l* 1562[a]      Clark, *USA*, pp. 23–5

*l* 1562[b]      Clark, *USA*, pp. 20–2

Plates      Clark 2

*l* 1563      Clark, *USA*, pp. 1–2

*l* 1564      Clark, *USA*, pp. 185–6

Plates      Facsimile of 1 page in B. W. Robinson, 'New Ms. Acquisitions for Chicago', *University of Chicago Magazine* XX (1929), 240–7

*l* 1566      J. M. Heer, 'Neue Griechische-Saidische Evangelienfragmente', *Oriens Christ* II (1912), 1–47 (and facsimile of part of Freiburg fragment)

*l* 1571      M. R. James, *A Descriptive Catalogue of the Maclean Collection of Mss in the Fitzwilliam Museum* (Cambridge, 1912), pp. 1–2

| | |
|---|---|
| *l* 1575 | K.Schüssler, 'Eine Griechisch-koptische Handschrift des Apostolas (*l* 1575 und 0129, 0203)', *ANTF* 3, pp. 218–65 |
| | W. Till, 'Papyrussammlung der Nationalbibliothek in Wien. Katalog der koptischen Bibelbruchstücke. Die Pergamente', *ZNW* 39 (1940), 45 |
| Plates | A & A 58 |
| *l* 1577 | Clark, *USA*, p. 276 |
| *l* 1578 | Clark, *USA*, pp. 278–9 |
| *l* 1579 | Clark, *USA*, pp. 322–3 |
| | M.W. Redus, *The Text of the Major Festivals of the Menologion in the Greek Gospel Lectionary*, Studies in the Lectionary Text II, 2 (Chicago, 1936) |
| *l* 1586 | Clark, *USA*, pp. 325–6 |
| *l* 1597 | Clark, *USA*, pp. 225–6 |
| *l* 1598 | Clark, *USA*, p. 261 |
| *l* 1599 | Clark, *USA*, pp. 229–31 |
| | Complete collation: see E.C. Colwell and D.W. Riddle (eds.), *Prolegomena to the Study of the Lectionary Text of the Gospels*, Studies in the Lectionary Text I (Chicago, 1933), pp. 81, 84–156 (cited as collation 'A') (see also *l* 1231) |
| Plates | Hatch, *Uncials*, LXVII |
| | Clark 41 |
| *l* 1600 | Clark, *USA*, pp. 259–61 |
| *l* 1602 | J.M. Heer, 'Zu den Freiburger griechische-saidischen Evangelienfragmenten', *Oriens Christ* III (1913), 141–2 (see *l* 1566) |
| | Henri Hyvernat, *Bibliothecae Pierpont Morgan Codices Coptici: photographice expressi* XI, *Evangeliarium Graeco-Sahidice*, 56 vols. with an Index Tabularum and an Index Pericoparum (Rome, 1922) |
| | Clark, *USA*, pp. 153–5 |
| *l* 1603 | E.A.W. Budge, *Coptic Biblical Texts in the Dialect of Upper Egypt* (London, 1912), pp. 249–55 |

| | |
|---|---|
| *l* 1604 | Published by P.E. Kahle, *Bala'izah* I (London, 1954), pp. 399–407 and plate |
| *l* 1605 | O.H.E. Burmester, 'The Bodleian Folio and Further Fragments of the Coptic–Greek–Arabic Holy Week Lectionary from Scetis', *Bull Soc Arch Copte* 17 (1963–4), 35–48 |
| *l* 1609 | Clark, *USA*, pp. 256–9 (and 2401[a]) |
| *l* 1610 | Clark, *USA*, pp. 276–7 |
| *l* 1611 | Clark, *USA*, p. 277 |
| *l* 1612 | Clark, *USA*, pp. 279–80 |
| *l* 1613 | Clark, *USA*, pp. 319–20 |
| *l* 1614 | Clark, *USA*, pp. 324–5 |
| *l* 1615 | Clark, *USA*, pp. 326–7 |
| *l* 1616 | Clark, *USA*, pp. 329–30 |
| *l* 1617 | Clark, *USA*, p. 330 |
| *l* 1518 | Clark, *USA*, 333–4 |
| *l* 1619 | Clark, *USA*, pp. 54–5 |
| *l* 1620 | Clark, *USA*, p. 60 |
| *l* 1621 | Collation by J.A. Nichols, Unpublished Th.M. thesis, Princeton Theological Seminary, 1954 |
| | Clark, *USA*, pp. 76–8 |
| *l* 1622 | Herbert T. Weiskotten, 'The Greek Evangelistary, a Study of Garret Ms. 5424 in the Princeton University Library', *American Library Institute Papers and Proceedings* (1917), 57–142 |
| | Collation by J.H. Houdeshel, Unpublished Th.M. thesis, Princeton Theological Seminary, 1950 |
| | Clark, *USA*, pp. 78–9 |
| *l* 1623 | Clark, *USA*, pp. 87–9 |
| *l* 1624 | Clark, *USA*, pp. 94–5 |
| *l* 1625 | Clark, *USA*, pp. 95–6 |
| *l* 1626 | Clark, *USA*, pp. 101–2 |
| *l* 1627 | Description and collation in Robert H. Daube, 'The Text of a Greek Manuscript in the Possession of Dr. L. Franklin Gruber, D.D., LL.D.', Unpublished M.A. thesis, University of Chicago, 1931 |

| | |
|---|---|
| | M.W. Redus, *The Text of the Major Festivals of the Menologion in the Greek Gospel Lectionary*, *Studies in the Lectionary Text* II, 2 (Chicago, 1936) |
| | Clark, *USA*, pp. 102–3 |
| | (See also *l* 1231: Colwell and Riddle, complete collation) |
| Plates | Clark 23 |
| *l* 1628 | Clark, *USA*, p. 104 |
| *l* 1629 | Clark, *USA*, pp. 347–8 |
| Plates | Clark 53 |
| | Hatch, *Uncials*, LXVIII |
| *l* 1632 | Clark, *USA*, pp. 152–3 |
| Plates* | |
| *l* 1634 | M.W. Redus, *The Text of the Major Festivals of the Menologion in the Greek Gospel Lectionary*, *Studies in the Lectionary Text* II, 2 (Chicago, 1936) |
| | H.R. Willoughby, *The Four Gospels of Karahissar* II (Chicago, 1936), pp. 102, 255 |
| | Clark, *USA*, pp. 159–61 |
| Plates* | |
| *l* 1635 | Clark, *USA*, pp. 162–6 |
| Plates | Vikan 62 |
| | Clark 31 |
| Plates* | |
| *l* 1636 | Clark, *USA*, p. 26 |
| *l* 1637 | Clark, *USA*, pp. 314–15 |
| *l* 1638 | Clark, *USA*, pp. 315–16 |
| *l* 1639 | Clark, *USA*, pp. 318–19 |
| *l* 1640 | Clark, *USA*, pp. 323–4 |
| *l* 1641 | Clark, *USA*, p. 324 |
| *l* 1642 | Clark, *USA*, pp. 261–3 |
| *l* 1642 | Collation by S.A. Cartledge (see *l* 1231: Colwell and Riddle) |

| | |
|---|---|
| *l* 1643 | Clark, *USA*, pp. 214–15 |
| *l* 1644 | Clark, *USA*, pp. 131–2 |
| *l* 1645 | H. A. Sanders, 'Some Greek Fragments in the Freer Collection', *JBL* XXXIV (1915), 191–2 (and *l* 1646, *l* 1647) |
| | Clark, *USA*, p. 207 |
| *l* 1646 | Clark, *USA*, p. 206 |
| | (See *l* 1645: Sanders) |
| *l* 1647 | Clark, *USA*, pp. 207–8 |
| | (See *l* 1645: Sanders) |
| *l* 1648 | Clark, *USA*, pp. 182–3 |
| *l* 1649 | |
| Plates* | |
| *l* 1650 | |
| Plates* | |
| *l* 1652 | D. I. Pallas, *Byzantisch-neugriechische Jahrbücher* 11 (Athens, 1934–5), p. δ |
| *l* 1653 | Pallas (as *l* 1652, pp. δ–έ) |
| *l* 1661 | E. Wellesz, *Kirchenmusikalisches Jahrbuch* 25 (Cologne, 1930), 9–24 and plates 1–4 |
| Plates* | |
| *l* 1662 | |
| Plates* | |
| *l* 1663 | Clark, *USA*, pp. 267–8 |
| *l* 1664 | Pallas (as *l* 1652, p. μδ–μζ) |
| *l* 1665 | Pallas (as *l* 1652 p. ξζ) |
| *l* 1666 | Pallas (as *l* 1652 p. ξή) |
| *l* 1671 | Clark, *USA*, pp. 6–7 |
| *l* 1672 | Clark, *USA*, p. 59 |
| *l* 1673 | Clark, *USA*, p. 12 |
| *l* 1674 | Clark, *USA*, pp. 268–9 |
| *l* 1675 | Clark, *USA*, p. 373 |
| *l* 1677 | Clark, *USA*, pp. 96–7 |
| *l* 1678 | Clark, *USA*, p. 336 |

*l* 1679

Plates

*l* 1679    Collation by J. Geerlings in appendix D to R.
Nevius, *The Divine Names in the Gospels*, *S & D*
XXX (Salt Lake City, 1967)

*l* 1681–*l* 1684 S.P. Lambros, Νέος Ἑλληνομνήμων 12 (1915),
129, 232–3, 358, 465 ff.

*l* 1692    E. Kurilas, *Theologia* 14 (Athens, 1936), 122–7

*l* 1693    (as *l* 1692)

*l* 1694    D.M. Sarros, Ὁ ἐν Κωνσταντινουπόλει Ἑλλ.
Φιλολογ. Σύλλογος 33 (1914), 101–2

*l* 1695    E. Ioannides, Ὁ ἐν Κωνσταντινουπόλει Ἑλλ.
Φιλολογ. Σύλλογος 3 (1868), 106–7

*l* 1696    N.I. Giannopulos, Νέος Ἑλληνομνήμων 18
(1924), 448–9

*l* 1697–*l* 1707 S.P. Lambros, Νέος Ἑλληνομνήμων 10 (1913),
401–14

*l* 1708    S.P. Lambros, Νέος Ἑλληνομνήμων 9 (1912), 311

*l* 1709    S.P. Lambros, Νέος Ἑλληνομνήμων 11 (1914), 53

Plates*

*l* 1710    N.A. Bees, Δελτίον τῆς ἱστορικῆς καὶ
ἐθνολογικῆς Ἑταιρείας τῆς Ἑλλάδος 9 (1926),
67–8

*l* 1711–*l* 1718 Ch. Chatze Stauru, *Byz Z* 21 (1912), 69–74

*l* 1719    Demetrios Kallimachos, Ἐκκλησιαστικὸς Φάρος
13 (1913), 244

*l* 1720    Th. Bolides, *Studi bizantini e neoellenici* 5 (Rome,
1939), 411–15 and plate 6

*l* 1721

Plates    Bolides (as *l* 1720), plate 4

*l* 1722    A. Papadapoulos–Kerameus, Ἱεροδολυμάτικη
Βιβλιοθήκη V (St Petersburg, 1915)

*l* 1727

*l* 1728    D.M. Sarros, Ὁ ἐν Κωνσταντινουπόλει Ἑλλ.
Φιλολογ. Σύλλογος 33 (1914), 59

*l* 1730   See Loparev (0235) and Beneševič (0235)

*l* 1731   (As for *l* 1730)

*l* 1732–*l* 1735 B. Conev, *Opis na rukopisitě i staropečatnitě knigi na Narodnata biblioteka v Sofija* I (Sofia, 1910), pp. 512–14

*l* 1733

Plates*

*l* 1736

Plates*

*l* 1736–*l* 1738 N. Camariano, *Biblioteca Academiei Române. Catalogul manuscriselor grecești* II (Bucharest, 1940), p. 39

*l* 1739   W. Till, *ZNW* 39 (1940), 41 (see also *l* 1575)

*l* 1740   V. de Falco, *Rivista Indo-Greco-Italica* 14 (Naples, 1930), 102–3

*l* 1741   Amélineau, *Notice*, pp. 372–3. Text, p. 407

*l* 1743

Plates   Turyn, *GB* 5; description p. 17

*l* 1745

Plates*

*l* 1746

Plates   Wilson 8

*l* 1748   J. L. Hylberg, 'Ein griechischer Evangeliar', *Byz Z* 20 (1911), 498–502

     (See also 250: Birdsall)

*l* 1750

Plates*

*l* 1754

Plates*

*l* 1757   V. Beneševič, *Catalogus codicum manuscriptorum Graecorum qui in monasterio S. Catharinae in monte Sina asservantur* I (St Petersburg, 1911), p. 118

*l* 1763–*l* 1771 Beneševič (as *l* 1757), III, 1 (1917), pp. 30, 31, 47, 304, 309, 310, 320

*l* 1790      S. P. Lambros, Catalogue of the Greek Manuscripts on Mt. Athos, II (Cambridge, 1900), p. 225

*l* 1791      N. A. Bees, 'Κατάλογος τῶν χειρογράφων ρωδίκων τῆς ἁγιωτάτης Μητροπόλεως 'Αργυροκάστρου', in 'Ακαδημία 'Αθηνῶν, 'Επετηρὶς τοῦ Μεσαιωνικοῦ 'Αρχείου 4 (1952), pp. 131–2

*l* 1792–*l* 1799   D. I. Palals, Κατάλογος χειρογράφων τοῦ Βυζαντινοῦ Μουσείου 'Αθηνῶν III (Athens, 1955), pp. 8, 14–15, 45–8, 63–4, 98, 102, 110

*l* 1800

Plates*

*l* 1805

Plates*

*l* 1808

Plates*

*l* 1813

Plates*

*l* 1816

Plates*

*l* 1826

Plates*

*l* 1836      A. Jacob, *Revue des bibliothèques* 9 (Paris, 1899), 373 and 378

*l* 1837      (as for *l* 1836)

*l* 1838      M. R. James, *The Western Mss in the Library of Trinity College, Cambridge* I (Cambridge, 1900), p. 548

*l* 1842

Plates      Lake and Lake VI, 238

*l* 1886

Plates      Plate 26 in Benaki exhibition catalogue (Δεκα Αἰωνες 'Ελληνικη Γραφης) (Athens, 1977)

*l* 1888

Plates      Plate 13 in Benaki exhibition catalogue (see *l* 1886)

*l* 1889

Plates          Plate 10 in Benaki exhibition catalogue (see *l* 1886)

*l* 1892

Plates          Plate 1 in Benaki exhibition catalogue (see *l* 1886)

*l* 1923

Plates*

*l* 1924

Plates*

*l* 1940

Plates          Turyn (1964), 70 and 180; description pp. 97 f.

*l* 1948

Plates*

*l* 1969

Plates*

*l* 1978

Plates*

*l* 1979

Plates*

*l* 1981

Plates*

*l* 1984          Described by P. Easterling, 'Greek Mss. in
                 Cambridge ...', *Transactions of the Cambridge
                 Bibliographical Society* 4 (Cambridge, 1966), 185 f.

*l* 1987          See Easterling (*l* 1984), 187 f.

*l* 2138

Plates          Plate of Colophon: Duke University *Library Notes*
                 51 and 52 (1985), 57

*l* 2178          L. Politis, *Hellenika* 24 (Athens, 1971), 38, 51 and
                 plate 8

*l* 2179          (as *l* 2178)

*l* 2209          K. Treu, 'N.T. Griechische Mss. in Weimar',
                 *Philologus* 117 (Wiesbaden, 1973), 113 – 23, esp. 117

*l* 2279          Described by B. M. Metzger, *Neotestamentica* 20
                 (Cape Town, 1986), 59

*l* 2280          Described by B. M. Metzger, *Neotestamentica* 20
                 (Cape Town, 1986), 59

For a study of twenty-five lectionaries see

Harry M. Buck, *The Johannine Lessons in the
Greek Gospel Lectionary, Studies in the Lectionary
Text of the Greek New Testament* (Chicago, 1958),
vol. 2, no. 4, pp. 68–75 (Lectionaries: 12, 32, 64,
69, 80, 151, 159, 183, 191, 219, 303, 333, 372, 374,
381, 847, 853, 1231, 1564, 1579, 1627, 1634, 1642,
1752, 1754) and J. Duplacy, 'Les Lectionnaires et
l'édition du Nouveau Testament Grec', in *Mélanges
bibliques* (Gembloux, 1970), 509–46. Reprinted in
J. Delobel (ed.), *Etudes de critique textuelle du
Nouveau Testament, Bibliotheca ephemeridum
theologicarum Lovaniensium* LXXVIII (Louvain,
1987), pp. 80–117

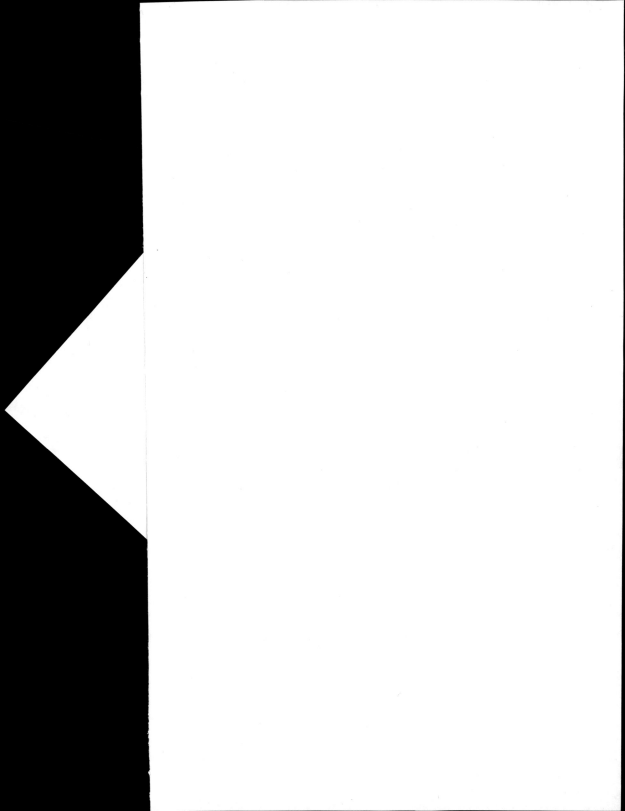

Demco, Inc. 38-293